DATE DUE		

Immigration

Look for these and other books in the Lucent
Overview series:

Abortion
Acid Rain
AIDS
Alcoholism
Animal Rights
The Beginning of Writing
Cancer
Dealing with Death
Death Penalty
Drugs and Sports
Drug Trafficking
Eating Disorders
Endangered Species
Energy Alternatives
Espionage
Extraterrestrial Life
Gangs
Garbage
The Greenhouse Effect
Gun Control
Hazardous Waste
The Holocaust
Homeless Children
Immigration
Ocean Pollution
Oil Spills
The Olympic Games
Organ Transplants
Ozone
Population
Prisons
Rainforests
Recycling
Smoking
Special Effects in the Movies
Teen Alcoholism
Teen Pregnancy
The UFO Challenge
Vietnam

Immigration

by Kelly C. Anderson

LUCENT
B·O·O·K·S

Library of Congress Cataloging-in-Publication Data

Anderson, Kelly, 1962-
    Immigration / by Kelly C. Anderson.
       p. cm. — (Lucent overview series)
    Includes bibliographical references and index.
    Summary: Discusses the immigrant presence in America, including
adjusting to life in America, illegal immigration, refugees, border disputes,
and the "salad bowl" versus the "melting pot."
    ISBN 1-56006-140-5
    1. United States—Emigration and immigration—Juvenile literature.
2. Immigrants—United States—Juvenile literature.   [1. United States—
Emigration and immigration. 2. Immigrants.]   I. Title. II. Series.
JV6455.A83   1993
325.73—dc20   92-44079
                                                     CIP
                                                      AC
Printed in the U.S.A.

Contents

АПТЕКА
ONE WA
BRIGHTON 5 ST
DONT WALK
WASH & DRY
B.Q. CKEN
Fried Chicken & Fish, Hamburger
MINI BLINDS
WINDOW SHADES
CUSTOM MADE
& READY MADE

Introduction

IMMIGRATION IS IMPORTANT to the United States. The unique American culture, economic system, and democratic politics are the result of past and present immigration. Sometimes, immigrant contributions are obvious. Sometimes, they are subtle, but even when the influences are not apparent or easy to trace, they exist and define who we are.

Immigrants in the United States

Immigrants can be found in almost every part of the United States, and they perform almost every kind of job. Immigrants are the presidents of large corporations, and immigrants fry hamburgers in restaurants. Immigrants are doctors, lawyers, real estate agents, and housewives. Sometimes, an immigrant such as actor Arnold Schwarzenegger or basketball star Patrick Ewing becomes rich and famous. Most of the time, immigrants are as diverse as any group of Americans.

Immigrant influence is visible in regional cuisines, politics, music, and economic activity. Sometimes, these regional differences stem from immigration that occurred more than one hundred years ago. For example, Scandinavian foods, music, and names are still common in the northern

(Opposite page) Immigrant and American customs and culture blend in many American cities and towns. In Brooklyn, New York, businesses beckon customers with signs in Russian and in English, and residents wear traditional wintertime Russian garb.

7

Midwest. Sometimes, regional differences are the result of more recent immigration. National fast-food chains now serve breakfast burritos in the American Southwest, where large numbers of Mexican immigrants have settled.

Immigrant presence is also evident when smaller groups of newcomers influence the area around their new homes. In Biloxi, Mississippi, recent Vietnamese immigration produced an increase in small fishing businesses and ethnic restaurants and grocers. Ethnic restaurants, in fact, are usually one of the more visible signs of an immigrant community. People from Thailand opened a restaurant in Saint Louis, Missouri, near a Jamaican jerk pit, down the street from an Ethiopian restaurant, and just a mile away from an Italian restaurant.

Immigrant presence can also be seen when immigrants bring new life and vigor to decaying neighborhoods. Cuban immigrants in Hudson County, New Jersey, are rebuilding and beautifying their neighborhood. They moved into an area considered run-down. When the Cuban immigrants first arrived, they enjoyed cheaper rents because of the poor conditions. As they became successful, they improved the buildings, cleaned up the streets, and restored beauty to a once neglected area.

New immigrants

Many people believe that immigration today is different from the immigration that occurred during the 1800s and early 1900s, when the United States was a new country and most of the immigrants came from Europe. Today, barely 10 percent of the immigrants come from Europe. More than 80 percent arrive from Asia and Latin America.

The motives behind today's immigration, however, are actually quite similar to those of the

Many Americans still celebrate the cultures of their immigrant past.

past. Immigrants tend to want to leave their native countries for similar reasons. Conditions such as overpopulation, few jobs, limited food, and poor living conditions have always motivated immigration and continue to do so.

Conditions in the United States encourage immigrants to select it as their new home. The hope of economic opportunity, political and social freedoms, and the chance to increase their skills and provide a better education for their children all attract immigrants.

An immigrant nation

The United States has always been a nation of immigrants. And each new ethnic group that joins the stream of immigrants has tended to create concern and controversy among the people who were already here. Sometimes, conflict arises over how quickly the immigrants adapt to the American life-style. Sometimes, the conflict is over the sheer number of immigrants allowed to enter. How we resolve these conflicts helps to define who Americans are and what Americans want their culture to be like. The answers often show that the United States benefits from immigration and that American society is, in fact, defined by immigrants.

1

From Many, One

WHEN PEOPLE TALK about immigration to the United States, many envision boatloads of immigrants approaching Ellis Island and viewing the Statue of Liberty for the first time. For hundreds of years, however, immigrants approached wild shores that were scarcely populated and often never even touched by humans before.

The first immigrants to this land walked here. People crossed the land bridge that no longer exists between Siberia and Alaska more than twenty thousand years ago. These people eventually walked to distant parts of the new land and settled throughout much of the present-day United States. When Europeans first discovered the Americas, they called these people Indians, and they are considered the only native Americans because they were already living here when European immigration began.

The first Europeans to travel to this land were not immigrants. Christopher Columbus, Henry Hudson, Sir Francis Drake, and other explorers did not plan to settle in the New World. The purpose of their exploration was to find trade routes. They instead discovered a lightly populated land plentiful with natural resources. This discovery disappointed some of the European kings and queens who were hoping to be rewarded with

(Opposite page) Christopher Columbus and other European explorers did not plan to settle in the New World. But others saw great potential for making a new life in this vast land.

11

gold and precious jewels. But this discovery was exciting to many people who saw the potential of settling a new land.

The first Europeans who came to the area that later became the United States were colonists. Immigrants leave their country to settle in another country. Colonists also leave their homeland to live in a new location, but their new place of residence is also governed by their native country. Colonial governments were established in the new land for the settlers, but these governments were controlled by the country's leaders in Europe. The British, French, Dutch, and Spanish all established colonies in the New World. By 1776, there were thirteen British colonies along the eastern seaboard.

The colonists of the New World brought their political, economic, and cultural institutions with them. The British brought a strong tradition of self-government. The men and women who colonized this country knew how to participate in government and to assume the authority for tak-

British colonists arrive in the New World. They brought many traditions with them including a strong tradition of self-government.

ing care of their business. This tradition of self-government, however, eventually caused conflict with Great Britain and led to the American Revolution and the creation of the United States of America.

The American Revolution

The founding of this country and its government was engineered by British immigrants using the skills of their culture. Although each immigrant group to enter the United States faces a different experience, each group uses the skills and intelligence of its members to contribute to the greater good of the new society. The country's motto, *e pluribus unum*, recognizes this cultural feature. Translated, the Latin motto means "out of many, one."

When the British colonists broke their political ties with Great Britain, they broke economic ties as well. The colonial economy was based on subsistence farming and the extraction and exportation of natural resources. It was illegal in most instances for the colonists to manufacture these natural resources. Instead, the raw materials were shipped back to England where they were made into commercial products. For example, the southern colonies grew large crops of cotton. The cotton was sent to England, and there it was spun into thread, woven into textiles, and made into garments. After the Revolution, the former colonists increased the manufacturing activity in the new country.

In addition to the people needed to produce the raw materials, thousands of workers were needed to manufacture these resources into products. The new Americans encouraged British immigrants to come to the new country and take full advantage of the economic potential. Paterson, New Jersey, a town that was intentionally created as a site for

Silk workers in Paterson, New Jersey, around 1900. Manufacturers imported thousands of immigrant workers to fill jobs in factories such as this one.

manufacturing activity in the mid-1700s, imported tens of thousands of skilled workers. When the silk industry was moved to Paterson, it imported the silk workers and managers from Manchester, England, as well as the needed machines and other equipment.

Citizenship

The framers of the U.S. Constitution recognized the importance of immigration. George Washington summarized his views in 1783. He said:

> The bosom of America is open to receive not only the opulent and respectable stranger but the oppressed and persecuted of all nations and religions; who we shall welcome to a participation of all our rights and privileges, if by decency and propriety of conduct they appear to merit the enjoyment.

Prior to the adoption of the Constitution, the states had each handled immigration issues independently. The Founding Fathers believed that immigration and naturalization should be handled in a consistent way and therefore gave Congress the power to enact legislation regarding these areas.

One of the remarkable features of American immigration policy has always been the availability of citizenship. Many countries allow immigrants to live and work in the country but do not extend the rights and privileges of citizenship. Congress passed its first law on how to become a citizen in 1790, requiring only that a person reside in the United States for two years. This law was amended several times in the country's first decade, at one time raising the residency requirement to fourteen years. Other provisions required immigrants to register as aliens. An alien is a foreign-born resident who has not yet become a citizen of the United States. Aliens were required to register until the law was changed in the 1980s and to file a declaration of their intent to seek citizenship, which eventually became an application that could be approved or denied. The residency requirement was lowered to its present five years in 1802.

Not only does the United States make citizenship possible for an immigrant but also grants civil rights to aliens before they become citizens. Civil rights and liberties are another important tradition in British political culture. In the United States, these rights were expanded to include greater claims to privacy and free speech. Individual rights were also extended to women and children and eventually to former slaves and international residents. Although aliens are not able to vote and are not eligible for certain government positions, they do receive substantially the same protection of their rights from the Constitution as do citizens.

American freedom

The high regard for individual liberty is a traditional reason why people immigrate to the United States. From the colonists who landed at Plymouth Rock seeking religious freedom to Hungarians seeking political asylum, or protection, in the 1950s, the United States has been perceived as a place where people have freedom. This ideal of freedom not only has a strong influence on American political institutions but also influences the economic culture. The United States is not only a land where immigrants are free to speak their mind but also one where they are free to earn a living the way they choose.

American freedom attracts immigrants from every part of the globe. Free speech, religious freedom, freedom to associate with whom they please, economic freedoms, and rights to equal protection and equal opportunity all attract immigrants to American shores. Many new immigrants find joy in common activities that other Americans have grown to take for granted. For example, Mary Antin emigrated from Eastern Europe to Boston as a small child. She wrote of her experiences in 1894:

> On our second day I was thrilled with . . . what this freedom of education meant. A little girl from across the alley came and offered to conduct us to school. My father was out, but we five between us had a few words of English by this time. We knew the word *school*. We understood. This child, who had never seen us till yesterday, who could not pronounce our names, who was not much better dressed than we, was able to offer us the freedom of the schools of Boston! No application made, no questions asked, no examinations, rulings, exclusions; no machinations, no fees. The doors stood open for every one of us. The smallest child could show us the way.

Populating the territory

Immigrants were essential for providing the population necessary to settle new land as the United States expanded westward. Immigrants

Immigrants found freedom in America but were also often confused and unsettled by the culture of their adopted country.

from Germany, Sweden, and Norway were extremely important in settling the middle section of the country. The American Southwest, which was part of Mexico until the Mexican-American War, also benefited from immigration. California was particularly attractive to immigrants from around the world when gold was discovered in the San Francisco area in 1849. Tens of thousands of people rushed to the Golden State.

California became the site of another wave of immigration in the 1870s during the building of the transcontinental railroad. The railroad was seen by many businesspeople as the final fulfillment of the long-anticipated trade route to the East. Boats from the Orient could deliver goods to San Francisco, where they would then be loaded onto the freight cars of the transcontinental line and shipped to the Northeast. The California railroad company hired thousands of Chinese

European immigrants crowd the deck of the transatlantic oceanliner S.S. Patricia *as they arrive in New York harbor in 1906.*

In the mid-1800s, immigrants from around the world flocked to California seeking their fortunes in the gold mines.

laborers to construct the railroad through the treacherous Sierra Nevada. The Chinese laborers were regarded as hard workers who did not complain about their conditions. Working long hours, the Chinese immigrants used hand tools to chip through the mountains, laying track at a phenomenal rate.

Many Chinese considered themselves sojourners rather than immigrants. A sojourner is like a traveler. A sojourner intends to remain in a place for a while to work but has plans to eventually return to the home country. For this reason, few Chinese were interested in adopting American culture. The Chinese were also restricted to living in certain areas by segregation laws. Most of the Chinese in the San Francisco area were required to live in one section of the city that became known as Chinatown. There were other Chinatowns in

California villages and cities that had attracted Chinese immigrants eager to take advantage of the gold rush, the railroad, and other opportunities.

The American citizens in California, however, began to resent the Chinese. The completion of the transcontinental railroad made it much cheaper and easier for people to move to California from the eastern United States. In the late 1870s, thousands of people moved to California. About the same time, a national depression in the economy limited the available jobs. Many of the white Californians became hostile to the Chinese workers who were hired instead because they were thought to be better laborers. Some of these Californians believed that native-born people should be given first consideration for jobs. These people became known as nativists. The nativists were influential in passing the first laws restricting immigration to the United States.

Opposition to immigration

The Industrial Revolution also encouraged new waves of immigration. Labor was in high demand

Many Chinese workers who labored on the railroads intended to stay only as long as they had work. But many never left, making their lives in legally sanctioned segregated communities.

Exhausted immigrants from eastern and southern Europe huddle for warmth on the deck of the oceanliner Westernland *as they wait to disembark at Ellis Island in New York.*

in the United States following the Civil War. People from throughout Europe began to immigrate to this country. Large numbers of new immigrants arrived from southern and eastern Europe, especially Italy, Greece, Poland, and Russia. These immigrants were more likely to be Catholic, Orthodox, or Jewish, rather than Protestant. Many of the new immigrants ate food that was unusual to the British-Americans. Their coloring was also often darker and distinguished them visually.

Strong anti-Catholic and anti-Semitic feelings were apparent in places such as Boston and New York where large numbers of immigrants had settled to take work in nearby industries. Some citizens began to oppose immigration to the United States because they believed that the people of this country should be relatively similar.

Some of these citizens formed a political party to oppose continued immigration, called the Know-Nothing party. Members of the Know-Nothing party were usually nativists, who believed that the native-born population of the United States had a privileged and superior right to the benefits of the country. The Know-Nothings became the American party and elected about seventy-five members across the country to Congress.

Restrictions

Samuel F. B. Morse was an inventor who ran for mayor of New York City as a nativist candidate in 1836 and lost. Morse was extremely skeptical of the newcomers to the United States:

> How is it possible that foreign turbulence imported by shiploads, that riot and ignorance in hundreds of thousands of human priest-controlled machines should suddenly be thrown into our society and not produce turbulence and excess? Can one throw mud into pure water and not disturb its clearness?

Together with the California nativists who opposed Chinese immigration, the Know-Nothings were able to impose the first limitations on immigration to the United States.

Despite growing resentment and restrictions against them, more than twenty million people immigrated to the United States between 1880 and 1914. Almost half of these immigrants came from southern and eastern Europe, while barely 40 percent arrived from northern and western Europe. Despite the fears of nativists, these immigrants—like those before and after them—did become part of the American human landscape. Many of these people arrived with greatly needed skills. Some came with the capital to start new businesses. They brought their preferences for religion, food, music, art, and literature with them.

Children worship at strange altars in an 1873 illustration that reflects public fears about foreign influences on daily life, children, and schools.

Their story is largely the story of how the United States became the modern, industrial society that it is today.

This great wave of immigration that was so essential in forming the U.S. economy and enhancing its culture came to a fairly abrupt halt in 1914. On June 28, in Austria-Hungary, Archduke Francis Ferdinand was assassinated, sparking the existing European political tensions into World War I. The war greatly reduced immigration to the United States. Many people who might have immigrated in peaceful times stayed to fight for their homeland or were unable to leave once the fighting began. The war was followed by a worldwide economic depression, known as the Great Depression. The U.S. economy suffered so badly from the depression that there were several years in which more people left the country than entered it. Before the depression was over, trouble had started again in Europe and by the early 1940s the United States had become involved in World War II. Between 1914 and 1950, from World War I to World War II, fewer than nine

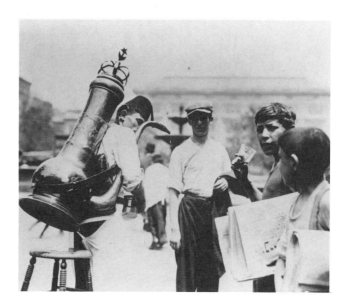

Immigrants were eager to adapt to American life yet they often retained their own traditions. A vendor sells cold drinks, Syrian-style, in New York about 1910.

million people immigrated to the United States.

These low rates of immigration continued after the war because the United States greatly restricted who was allowed to enter. From 1924 to 1965, immigration was based on a quota system. The Congress that created these restrictive laws wanted new immigrants to be from the same ethnic groups that had originally contributed to the U.S. population. Congress decided to allow each country a quota, or percentage of the total immigration, based on the percentage of immigrants from that country who arrived in the United States prior to 1890. By basing the quotas on the population of twenty-five years earlier, Congress excluded large numbers of people who would have liked to immigrate to the United States but whose countries did not have a long tradition of sending immigrants here.

The new immigrants

This law especially affected potential immigrants from southern and eastern Europe but also made it virtually impossible for new immigration from Asia and Africa. When the law was revised in 1965, immigrants from the excluded areas of the globe began to arrive in the United States in greater numbers. They are often considered the "new immigrants."

Both new and old immigrants have formed the basic institutions and culture of the United States. Immigrants created the political structure of the country and developed its economy. Immigration has been so important to the United States that it is not possible to separate the general contributions of immigrants from those of the native-born. Whether a citizen is born to a family that immigrated generations ago or born to a family that recently arrived, that citizen has the chance to play an equal role in advancing this society.

2

Adjusting to American Culture

COMING TO THE UNITED STATES is often an exciting, hope-filled journey for immigrants. The experience of arriving in a new country and beginning a new life is also filled with many challenges. One of the biggest challenges faced by new immigrants is adjusting to American culture.

The United States welcomes immigrants to its shores, but it also demands that they adapt and conform to the culture once they arrive. Acculturation is the process of change newcomers undergo as they adapt. Acculturation can also occur when the culture itself undergoes changes as a result of contact with the newcomers.

The process of acculturation is different for everyone. Immigrants to the United States come from more than one hundred different countries and speak many different languages and dialects. They have been shaped by hundreds of different ethnic influences. Even two immigrants who come from the same town are likely to have different experiences when they arrive in the United States. Different personalities and ways of coping with change will make the process unique for each new arrival.

(Opposite page) A new world opens for young immigrants in school. They study reading, writing, and arithmetic but also learn a great deal about American culture from their classmates.

Immigrants face many challenges, especially learning English, adapting to American culture, and establishing a work life. The challenges may be difficult and numerous, but hundreds of thousands of new immigrants successfully meet these challenges each year.

Social adjustment

Some immigrants are well prepared for the transition to American life. Immigrants from the Philippines, for example, are often able to adapt relatively easily because schools and businesses often use English in the Philippines and the colleges and universities are based on American models. Degrees from Philippine colleges are often accepted by American employers without additional training. U.S. military bases in the Philippines have maintained a large American population there for decades, keeping the Philippine people in constant contact with American culture. Along with Mexico and China, the Philippines is one of the most common countries of origin among immigrants.

Many immigrants, however, find adjustment difficult and painful. The Hmong tribal people from Laos have a rural, agricultural background. Most have never even met an American before they arrive in this country. They do not know English, and most do not have any formal education. It is uncomfortable for them to work close to others because of a cultural taboo against touching. The Hmong, and other groups with a rural background, tend to take much longer to adjust to life in the United States. They take longer to find jobs, and their first jobs are usually low-paying, unskilled positions. Hmong adjustment to American culture has been so stressful that it is linked with Sudden Death Syndrome, also called SUDS, which has killed many young Hmong males in

Adjustment to American life is more difficult for some than others. It has been especially hard for the rural Hmong people of Laos. A Hmong boy poses for a photograph in his new home.

the United States. Many surviving Hmong believe these young men died of homesickness.

One of the biggest adjustments the Hmong have had to make is learning to make decisions independently. Raleigh Bailey, who runs a high school adjustment program for the Hmong, said, "Our biggest challenge is to get the Hmong to make decisions for themselves." This is because the tribal leader made all the decisions in Hmong culture, determining what crops a family would grow or who could marry. Bailey introduces independent decision making and democracy to the students:

> We have the students vote on all sorts of issues— from what day they'll play kickball, to whether they'll wear yellow or green tags to a special event. That way, they begin to learn that everyone has a right to voice an opinion and that, in a pluralistic, democratic society, the majority rules.

Many immigrants find adjustment is made easier by living near other immigrants from the same country. It is a relief for many to relax using their native language and to talk to people who find their thoughts and habits familiar rather than foreign. These friends will often help the new immigrant in his or her first few months in the United States.

Regions that draw a particular group of immigrants are sometimes referred to as magnets. Most magnet communities have large immigrant populations that attract more immigrants from the same country of origin. Dearborn, Michigan, for example, attracts a large number of immigrants from the small Middle Eastern country of Yemen. Yemeni immigrants in Dearborn have found successful employment in the automobile factories and encourage friends and family members who immigrate to join their community. The transition from Yemen to Michigan is softened by the pres-

Traces of a strong immigrant presence are visible on a downtown Los Angeles street, where a vendor sells Mexican-style frozen fruit bars and day laborers wait for work.

ence of other Yemeni immigrants. The West Indian population of Baltimore, Maryland, similarly draws a large number of immigrants from Jamaica, Trinidad, and other Caribbean nations.

Los Angeles could be considered the biggest magnet city in the country. It attracts thousands of newcomers each year to its large Chinese, Korean, and Latino neighborhoods. Asians, whose immigration was severely limited before 1965, overwhelmingly chose California as their new home when they began to immigrate in large numbers after 1965.

Language and education

For many immigrants, learning the language is the biggest problem in successfully adapting to American culture. In most of the United States, it is difficult to accomplish even simple, everyday chores without some knowledge of English. It is hard to buy groceries, order food at a restaurant, ask for directions, or identify street signs without English. Most jobs require English fluency, and most people are expected to complete a job application in English before even being considered for that job.

English is so important to coping with every aspect of American life that not knowing English can be terrifying. Ya Thong and his family are from Laos. When they arrived in the United States, they spoke only Lao and French. Ya Thong said the whole family was frightened by the experience of not being able to communicate. "Everybody scared. In the daytime we are scared to go outside because we cannot speak English and we may get lost. We stay in house and stare at each other."

Being able to communicate is such an important part of the process of adapting to a new culture that many immigrants say that learning English was a turning point for them. "Without English, everything seemed hard," said Agneska, originally from Poland, "but with English, everything got much easier." Learning English makes it easier to adapt to American ways and values, which are reflected in the language. Getting a job

Many immigrants know that language is the key to adapting to any culture. A seventeen-year-old Salvadoran immigrant works on his English at school.

Immigrant and American-born students often learn from each other as they form new friendships in school.

and "thinking like an American" are often only possible after the immigrant begins using English. Immigrants understand this challenge, and most work hard to learn English.

Learning English

Sister Anne Wisda helped to resettle more than five thousand Cambodians sponsored by the Catholic Diocese of Oklahoma City. Sister Anne stressed that among the many challenges of adapting to American culture, learning English is one of the most time-consuming. "At night and on weekends they study English. Learning English is hard for them, maybe the hardest thing of all. But most are trying their very best to learn," she said.

Immigrant children must also learn English, and many do so faster than their parents. Studies by linguists show that children in general are better able to master a second or third language than are adults. Immigrant children also have the added advantage of attending schools with native-born children, where they practice their English skills. Many studies show that immigrant children succeed as well as native-born children in school, especially on standardized tests.

In some cases, immigrants outperform the native-born. Freda Skirvin is an administrator at a school with a large Asian student body in a suburb of Washington, D.C. Skirvin said many of their immigrant children actually did better than the general student body:

> Most Asian students I have seen bring an unusual degree of hard work, concentration, and interest to their studies. I don't know whether it is self-discipline, ambition, family expectations or all those things, but the result is academic accomplishment well above the average.

Success in school may be more difficult for

students who arrive in their teens, however. Loi Mai is an Asian-American who arrived from Vietnam in 1989 at the age of sixteen. Loi Mai performed extremely well in math and was proficient in other subjects, but his poor English skills held him back. Loi Mai was still in high school when he was nineteen, with only about two-thirds of the credits he needed to graduate. Loi Mai was so embarrassed by this situation that he considered quitting school and giving up on his dreams for the future. He went back only after speaking to older immigrants who convinced him that he should stay to learn because the education and the English would be important for his life in the United States.

Young immigrants

Immigrant children adjust to American culture more rapidly than their parents largely because of their school experience. Elementary and secondary education in the United States teaches both immigrant and native-born children basic concepts about the government, the economy, and other social organizations. English is spoken, and formal written English is taught to all students. Contact with their peers teaches children about trends, fashion, and pop culture in addition to the information they learn in the classroom.

Ya Thong, originally from Laos, said adjustment is harder for adults, who will always remember and feel connected to their native land. "With the children, of course, it is different. They will become Americans very quickly. Once they start to school, you can almost see it happening before your eyes," Ya Thong said.

This rapid change in the children sometimes creates conflict for immigrant parents who want their children to become Americans but also desire that their children know about and respect the

32

culture of their heritage. Sometimes, immigrant children feel embarrassed when their parents urge them to wear traditional clothes or take traditional foods to school for lunch. A survey of Koreans in Los Angeles found that conflict between parents and children was common.

Many of these children are torn between their American desires and trying to please their parents. Korean immigrant Marcia Choo, for example, cannot ignore her father's expectations for her to become a professional—a doctor or a lawyer. Her father's dream was part of the reason why the family immigrated. She explained that this is a constant conflict in her life: "My father and I fight about this all the time. I have this overwhelming sense of burden and responsibility." Despite these conflicts, many immigrant children adjust to American life while maintaining a link to their parents' past.

Employment

Most immigrants move to the United States for economic opportunity. Many immigrants find better jobs in the United States than they would have ever had in their home country. They may be engineers, nurses, business managers, mechanics, and manufacturing workers. Some immigrants, however, face considerable hardships in the American job market. Some may have left good-paying, respected positions but find that in the United States they must take low-paying jobs that do not require much skill or education. They may be dishwashers, maids, cashiers, or clerical workers.

Immigrants who used to have good jobs are often saddened and frustrated when they must start over in the United States. Homa Ehsan, for example, was the first woman newscaster in Iran, and she feels that she lost prestige and fame when she

Strained relations between parents and children sometimes result from the changes confronting immigrant families.

left her country. Today, Homa Ehsan produces programs for Iranian radio in Los Angeles, but she has not forgotten the initial pain of her move to the United States:

> It was very difficult. I had to go through a lot. The first pain comes when you realize that whatever you have done, whatever you have made, whatever you have been before—it's gone. I was a famous personality in my country. I was called the Barbara Walters of Iran. I didn't even have to introduce myself on the telephone. As soon as I would say hello, they would call my name. Here I had to spell my name and pronounce my name, and insist that I'm not a terrorist.

Many immigrants find they have to take multiple jobs in order to provide adequate support for their families in the United States. The Yi family is typical. Ki Chong Yi was a heavy equipment operator in Korea. These jobs are generally high-paying positions in the United States, but Ki Chong Yi could not get a job in this field because of his limited English skills and local regulations for such operators. Ki Chong Yi worked part-time as a car mechanic, had a full-time job as a janitor for a public school, and filled in as needed on the cleaning staff at Fort Belvoir in Washington, D.C. His wife, Hyo Cha Yi, worked two jobs. She cleaned at Fort Belvoir from six in the morning to one in the afternoon, and she was a janitor at Bucknell Elementary School from three in the afternoon until eleven o'clock at night.

New businesses

Many immigrants start new businesses. Sometimes, these new businesses are directly related to work and other experience gained back home. When Vietnamese newcomers arrived in Biloxi, Mississippi, many took jobs with the established fishing businesses. Many of these Vietnamese had worked in the fishing industry in their native

Vietnamese fishermen prepare their net for a day of shrimping in Gulfport, Mississippi. The Mississippi gulf coast is home to a community of Vietnamese immigrants.

land, so they had valuable skills to offer their new employers. When they learned the American way of business, many of these Vietnamese newcomers began their own fishing businesses and hired family members to work for them. Their tremendous success caused some problems with competitors who claimed the Vietnamese engaged in unfair practices, including learning inside business information, fishing and shrimping earlier and later hours than the Americans, and fishing in bad weather. The Vietnamese in Biloxi eventually cooperated with their new neighbors and adopted the local fishing customs.

Whether immigrants work multiple jobs, open their own businesses, or hold professional positions, they are generally successful at adapting to the American economy. One study showed that immigrant families on average earn more than native-born families of a similar age within ten years of their arrival. This finding may be misleading. Immigrant families tend to have more family members employed than native-born families. For example, an immigrant family may have a father, mother, grandmother, and oldest brother who are all full-time wage earners living in the same household.

But high family incomes do demonstrate that over a short amount of time, immigrants are able to adjust to American culture and economic life well enough to function at jobs and provide support for their families. Sometimes, immigrant economic success is phenomenal. For example, more than two hundred former Cuban exiles are today millionaires and have started new businesses that have helped the local economy, especially in Florida and New Jersey.

A shop in one of Miami's Cuban neighborhoods. Many immigrants prosper by starting their own businesses.

Citizenship

The ideal adjustment to American culture is becoming a citizen. More than 270,000 people became naturalized U.S. citizens in 1990. The most common countries of origin were the Philippines with 25,936 successful applications, Vietnam with 22,027, and Mexico with 17,664.

Immigrants may be eligible to become citizens after they have lived in the United States continuously for five years. This process is called naturalization, and it has several requirements. Natu-

For many immigrants, citizenship represents the final step to becoming an American. A group of immigrants takes the oath of American citizenship.

3

Illegal Immigration

THE UNITED STATES is a beacon to potential immigrants around the world but admits only a small portion of those immigrants. Millions of people from such countries as Mexico, China, Vietnam, Ethiopia, Ireland, Poland, Nigeria, Haiti, and Peru would like to move to the United States, but the country does not have room for them all. Many come anyway as illegal aliens. Successful illegal immigration is estimated by some to be as high as twice the amount of legal immigration.

Illegal population

Congress limits total immigration to about 700,000 newcomers annually. Some of these spaces are reserved for immigrants in specific categories, such as those with money to invest in businesses or those with special job skills. Most of the spaces are given to immigrants who are related to U.S. citizens. These spaces are shared by immigrants from all over the globe on a percentage basis. Each country can send a limited number of immigrants, determined by a formula that is calculated by the State Department. China, for example, was allowed to send 25,620 family-

(Opposite page) Hundreds of people illegally cross the U.S.-Mexico border daily. Many slip by the watchful eyes of U.S. Border Patrol agents but many others do not. A group of illegal aliens in handcuffs follows Border Patrol agents in San Diego, California.

39

based immigrants in 1992, which was 7 percent of the total for that category.

Many countries are not allotted enough spaces to meet the demand for immigration. Mexico, for example, has many more applicants for immigration to the United States than there are spaces available. When the limits are met for a given country, additional applicants may be put on a waiting list. In some countries, such as Mexico, waiting lists may be as long as ten years for regular legal immigration to the United States. When demand for immigration is higher than the spaces available, potential immigrants sometimes decide to move anyway, without approval, as illegal aliens.

Numbers vary

There is no exact count of illegal aliens in the United States. Estimates range widely. The Census Bureau estimated the 1990 illegal population at 2 to 3.5 million, although some researchers believe the actual numbers may be as high as 5 or 6 million. The illegal population is predicted to double by the year 2000, if the same number of illegal aliens continues to enter the country each year.

Researchers estimate anywhere from 100,000 to 1 million aliens illegally enter the United States each year in order to live here permanently. Many illegal aliens also leave each year, for a variety of reasons. Aliens may fail to find a job, they may have saved enough money to return home, or they may have returned home for a visit and not been able to get back to the United States. The Census Bureau estimates that about 200,000 illegal aliens successfully enter each year.

Most illegal aliens are from Mexico, Central America, and the Caribbean. In fact, more than 93 percent of all illegal aliens apprehended by the Immigration and Naturalization Service (INS) in

1990 were Mexican. The INS discovered 4,661 Mexicans who worked in agricultural jobs; 7,544 in trades, service jobs, and other industries; and 865,739 seeking employment. Illegal aliens also come from Canada, South America, and most other regions of the world.

Illegal immigrants want to live in the United States for most of the same reasons that other immigrants come here. They seek a life with democratic freedoms and the opportunity to find a job or start a business. For the most part, illegal aliens would have come to the United States as legal immigrants if there were enough spaces for them. For those who decide to come anyway, the stress of immigrating, the risks of illegal entry, the fear of getting caught, low-wage jobs, and small or shared living quarters are still preferable to facing the bleak possibilities of their native land.

Mexico, for example, had a population boom during the 1960s and 1970s, and as a result, there are more young people in Mexico looking for their

Like legal immigrants, illegal immigrants seek a better life for themselves and their families. A poor shantytown outside Mexico City offers little hope for its residents.

first job than ever before. At the same time, as hundreds of thousands of young adults are trying to start their careers, Mexico has faced difficult economic times and even fewer jobs than usual are available. The increased population also burdened many large Mexican cities, such as the capital, Mexico City, and living conditions have worsened as the population increased. The result is that Mexico has had far more people who want to emigrate, or leave the country, each year than will be approved to come to the United States. Facing the very real possibility that they will never find work in Mexico or that if they do, it will not pay enough to support their families, many Mexicans have decided to risk the journey north.

Illegal entry

This journey takes many illegal aliens to the U.S. border. The two-thousand-mile-long border with Mexico extends from Texas to California and passes along the borders of New Mexico and Arizona. For most of its stretch, a person can

The fence that separates the United States and Mexico is little more than a symbolic barrier between the two nations.

simply walk across the border. The Texas-Mexico border is formed by the Rio Grande, a river that for most of its length can be waded across and is not a serious barrier. The majority of illegal immigrants cross this huge southern border to enter the United States. The people who cross there are primarily Mexican, but thousands also come from Colombia, Ecuador, Costa Rica, Jamaica, and Haiti. In smaller numbers, people arrive from virtually every country in the Caribbean and throughout Central and South America.

Tens of thousands of people illegally enter across the southern border, primarily in and near San Diego, California, and El Paso, Texas. The crossing is fraught with tremendous risks and dangers. Desert territory extends for hundreds of miles on both sides of the border, and actually walking across the border would take weeks of hard physical labor. Few towns or people exist on either side of the border for most of the stretch between Mexico and the United States.

The majority of illegal immigrants cross into the United States along the country's southern border.

"If not today . . ."

The tall fences that separate Mexico and the United States, particularly in heavily populated areas, are full of people-size holes that immigrants use to cross, especially at night. Each day in El Paso, for example, many immigrants sneak through the fence, crossing the river by foot, and catch a late-night train out of El Paso or hide among legal immigrants within the city. The Border Patrol, the branch of the INS that guards the border, captures and returns hundreds of people every day but cannot possibly locate and return all of the illegal immigrants, who greatly outnumber the officers.

Every day in Tijuana, Mexico—one of the busiest border crossings in the world—several hundred or even thousands of people gather on the

southern border to attempt an illegal crossing. Many wait for nightfall to attempt the crossing. Spectators sometimes watch the Border Patrol chase the people who try to cross, often cheering for the potential immigrants to outrun their pursuers. They hope the border crossers will make it because it gives them hope that they, too, will be successful when they attempt the crossing. Optimism tends to run high among the people waiting to cross the border. They have a saying, "If not today, tomorrow," that reflects both the hope that they will succeed and the recognition that many are caught and must try many times before making it to the other side.

Some illegal crossers have enough money to hire someone to smuggle them into the United States. These smugglers are called coyotes, and they are one of the many dangers illegal aliens face. Coyotes may charge from one hundred to several thousand dollars to transport someone over the border. The Border Patrol arrested more than twenty thousand coyotes in 1990 and discovered more than seventy thousand aliens being smuggled by coyotes into the United States.

Smugglers

Coyotes have been accused of many human atrocities. In addition to their primary illegal activity of smuggling humans for high fees, they may steal or extort additional money from these aliens. Some reports have accused coyotes of leaving aliens penniless in the Southwest desert with no food or water and no sense of direction. Many have died after putting their trust in these "guides" across the border.

José Sanchez* entered the United States illegally at the California-Mexico border. Sanchez is originally from El Salvador. He flew to Mexico City on a tourist visa, then hitchhiked to Tijuana and took a taxi to the border. He bribed Mexican police and border guards along the way. Next, he hired a coyote.

The coyote helped Sanchez cross the border through a huge drainage tunnel. The coyote then put Sanchez in the trunk of a car for the drive to Los Angeles. The coyote then extorted money from Sanchez by threatening to turn him over to the INS. The coyote held Sanchez for several weeks before Sanchez learned the coyote was also an illegal alien. At that point, Sanchez realized the coyote would not endanger his own status by turning him in. Sanchez convinced the coyote to release him and then used the last of his hidden money to catch a plane to New York City, where he lives and works illegally today.

The desire to cross the border is so great that even at heavily guarded official border crossings,

*Author's note: José Sanchez is a fictitious name.

A woman waits for a handout between lines of cars crossing from Mexico into the United States at San Ysidro, California. This stretch of border is the world's busiest international crossing.

people may openly defy the Border Patrol. In the 1990s, a new tactic evolved to avoid the Border Patrol—running against automobile traffic at checkpoints to get into the United States. This action is risky for pedestrians, who might be hit and killed by cars, and creates an additional road hazard for the drivers. The tactic worked, though, and many got through the congested traffic to the United States. And because it worked for some, others will probably continue to try it in the future.

Life-style

Of the unknown thousands or even millions who cross the border illegally each year, many are caught and returned to their countries. The rest make their way to cities throughout the United States and begin their new life. Like regular immigrants, they find jobs, start families, and adjust to the culture. Unlike regular immigrants, though, the fear of deportation is a constant worry.

Fear of being caught limits the social life, economic opportunity, and freedom of illegal aliens. Like regular legal immigrants, illegal aliens face the challenge of adjusting to American culture,

Mexicans illegally cross the Rio Grande River into El Paso, Texas. The man in front, whose face is not visible, makes his living transporting people across the river on rafts.

but they do so with the fear of discovery. They may be more hesitant to make friends with coworkers and other strangers, which may increase the time it takes to learn English and begin other adjustments to American life.

Illegal immigrants do not have permission to work in the United States. Many illegal immigrants accept work from business owners who pay low wages and do not care if a person is in the country illegally. Some illegal aliens find seasonal cash work in a variety of farming operations, doing things like picking fruit, growing vegetables, and harvesting cranberries, tomatoes, or grapes. Many times, they find work as unskilled or semiskilled manufacturing laborers, often working on assembly lines putting together things like small appliances or packaged foods. The garment industry has traditionally hired immigrants to work as long as fourteen or sixteen hours a day for pay below the minimum wage.

At risk

Working conditions at such factories are sometimes below safety standards. As a result, an illegal alien is likely to work more hours than law allows, for lower wages than are legal, and in places that put the worker's health and safety at risk. Illegal aliens are less likely to complain about bad working conditions or low wages for fear of being turned in to the INS. Some employers even turn such fears into threats, although abuses of this kind are seldom reported to anyone.

Not all illegal aliens work at the lowest-paying jobs. Some find work in much higher-paying fields, such as the construction industry or skilled manufacturing. Maria, for example, took a job at a garment factory below minimum wage when she first arrived illegally in New York. After she established a work history, she was able to get another job with another clothing factory that did not know she was working illegally and that paid above the minimum wage. But even when illegal immigrants approach a middle class life-style, they live with the risk that they could be discovered and deported.

Deportation would be a major setback for most illegal aliens, especially the ones who have been in the United States for a long time. Many of these people support families back in their native country. Without their American income, their families would suffer. Carlos, for example, came to the United States illegally because the one hundred dollars he earned each month in Guatemala City was not enough to support himself and his sister. Working in New York City, Carlos is able to send more than one hundred dollars a month back to his sister in Guatemala. If he is caught, they will both lose their income. Carlos says he fears being discovered, and he buys

A Mexican girl watches as U.S. Border Patrol agents detain her parents. She and her family were sent back to their home in Tijuana, Mexico.

medicinal herbs to keep himself healthy and to avoid doctors and hospitals.

Many illegal aliens use all of their life savings, and often the life savings of their families, to pay for getting to the United States. To lose that investment would be devastating for most because they could not afford to start over again. Some illegal aliens may have fled their country's violence, and immigrants from many places in Central America may fear for their lives if they are deported. Jorge, for example, an illegal alien from El Salvador, said he would return to his home on his own if it were safe for him to do so.

Illegal aliens create a new life for themselves in the United States. The longer they are in the United States, the more likely they are to get married or have children. Anyone born in the United States, including children of illegal aliens, is a U.S. citizen. The ties of illegal aliens increase the longer they live in the United States. For some, these ties may lead to legal status. For many, these ties mean that more is at stake with the risk of discovery.

Concerns about illegal immigrants

Illegal immigrants, like regular immigrants, are most likely to live in California, Texas, New York, and Illinois. As many as one in three live in the Los Angeles-Long Beach area, which had more than twice the illegal population of all of Texas. Other metropolitan areas with large illegal populations include Anaheim-Santa Ana in California, Houston, New York City, and Chicago.

Large illegal populations create huge burdens on community services and social welfare programs. Illegal aliens are often not counted by the census and, therefore, are not included when the federal government decides how much money to grant to cities, counties, and states to provide certain services.

Census figures are often used to distribute public money. Illegal aliens may not respond to the census, but the Census Bureau does estimate illegal populations in given areas. Areas with large illegal alien populations will receive some additional money to pay for government services but often not enough. In some places, these estimates are too low, and the extra costs of education and health care may not be covered. When this happens, all people served, including the legal immigrants and native-born, may get inferior services.

A heavy strain

The two services that consistently seem most affected by illegal immigration are education and medical care. The U.S. Supreme Court ruled in 1982 that local public school districts must provide education for all school-age children, including the children of illegal aliens. Local schools depend largely on state and federal funds to operate, so taxpayers bear the burden of additional schoolchildren. Larger numbers of students may mean hiring additional teachers, running additional buses, and even building additional schools. Sometimes, children of illegal aliens have special needs and require remedial education or bilingual education, for example, which are costly to provide.

Hospitals that receive a large part of their operating costs from government funds are usually required to serve all people who need health services, regardless of the patient's ability to pay. Many illegal aliens do not have health insurance coverage. Most illegal aliens avoid government health plans, such as Medicaid, because they fear that signing up for such programs would lead to their discovery. Like other people who lack health coverage, many illegal aliens do not seek medical care until their situation is critical and generally more costly to the taxpayer.

The illegal population is not only large in some cities but growing at a more rapid rate than the rest of the population. A rapid growth rate can create its own stresses on a city. Every month, demand increases for housing, jobs, education, transportation, utilities, and health care. Living conditions may deteriorate until area housing and basic services can catch up with the growing population.

Some people resent the illegal aliens and their negative impact on the community. On the other hand, towns with large immigrant populations can benefit from a rich cultural diversity and offer all residents a broader spectrum of life to experience.

Solutions

Many citizens are shocked by the large numbers of illegal aliens who enter the United States. Many citizens are angry that borders and laws are so openly defied. They believe that enforcement must be stronger to keep out illegal aliens. The American Immigration and Control Foundation holds this view. "Uncontrolled immigration threatens the future security and prosperity of our nation," the foundation says. "More than two million illegal aliens stream across our poorly guarded borders each year. These huge numbers, greater than at any time in our history, are more than our nation can assimilate and support."

Some citizens have urged better border enforcement through increases in the number of Border Patrol officers. Others have suggested bigger barriers along the border. Still others have urged strict employer sanctions to limit the job opportunities for illegal immigrants.

Congress reacted to these concerns and suggestions by passing the 1987 Immigration Reform and Control Act. Supporters believed this law

Crossing the U.S.-Mexico border is sometimes as easy as hopping a fence.

would be a significant step toward gaining control of America's borders and stopping the increase in the illegal population. One part of the law granted amnesty, or a pardon, for many illegal aliens already in the United States. Congress hoped that amnesty would reduce the size of the illegal population. (More than three million people received legal immigration status under this program.) The law tried to prevent future illegal immigration by creating employer sanctions, which were supposed to make it more difficult for illegal aliens to find work.

Employer sanctions punish businesses that hire illegal aliens. The law is intended to stop the main motivation behind illegal immigration. Many citizens believe that as long as employers are willing to hire illegal workers, then the workers will try to cross the border illegally. More than 80 percent of the one million illegal aliens apprehended by the INS in 1990 say they entered the country to find jobs.

Employer sanctions

Many employers dislike this law because it puts them in the position of regulating and enforcing immigration policies. The United States requires employers to verify the citizenship or legal immigration status of every new employee they hire. This creates additional paperwork and other expenses for employers, many of whom complain that they could save this time and money if the United States enforced its immigration policy effectively.

Many immigrants dislike employer sanctions because they fear it causes prejudice against all immigrants. Latino groups—who represent immigrants and native-born citizens—are especially fearful that the law encourages employers to discriminate against them, since most illegal aliens

"Oh! say, can you see, by the dawn's early light/ What so proudly we hailed at the twilight's last gleaming?/ Whose broad stripes and bright stars, through the perilous fight/ O'er the ramparts we watched were so gallantly streaming?/ And the rockets' red glare, the bombs bursting in air/ Gave proof through the night that our flag was still there./ Oh! say, does that star-spangled banner yet wave/ O'er the land of the free and the home of the brave?...Can I go now?"

are Latino.

In addition to employer sanctions, many citizens want stronger enforcement at the southern border with Mexico, the location of the country's biggest enforcement problem. The Border Patrol is often criticized for being too small a force to combat such a large number of immigrants crossing a two-thousand-mile border. Congress increased the Border Patrol by one thousand officers in 1990, raising the total to thirty-six hundred, but some critics believe as many as ten times that number of officers is needed to prevent illegal entries.

Lights and walls

Citizens have also suggested a wide variety of physical barriers or structures to at least make crossing the border a challenge. The current border fence is easily cut through and has actually been bulldozed away in some places. One citizen group wanted to replace the border fence with a tall concrete wall, which could not be cut through and would be harder to go over than a fence. The U.S. Army announced a plan in 1992 to place floodlights along the border fence in San Diego to make it harder for aliens to make night crossings undetected.

Many citizens support these efforts to gain control of U.S. borders, but many others think it is not enough. The problem of illegal immigration goes deeper than border walls and bright lights, these people say. Their view is that the waves of illegal immigrants will stop only when economic disparities between the United States and its neighbors to the south have been addressed. "Efforts to stop things at the border in the past have been Band Aid solutions," says University of Texas sociologist Frank Bean. "It is hard to see how this will be any different."

4

Refugees

THE UNITED STATES admits large numbers of immigrants each year, but it also welcomes another group of newcomers called refugees. Immigrants choose to leave their native country, while refugees are forced out of their homeland. Refugees are not safe in their native land, usually because of violent conditions, such as war, or because their native government has threatened them because of their actions or beliefs.

Originally, the U.S. government did not treat refugees differently or count them separately. There was no need for a special category for refugees until the United States put limits on immigration in the twentieth century. Refugees are specially admitted because their situation is considered so grave that keeping them out would be immoral. The United States first provided special admission in 1948 for more than half a million European refugees who lost their homes, and often their countries, during World War II.

Communist governments took control of many Eastern European countries in the decades following World War II, a time when the United States and the Soviet Union were engaged in the cold war. Most communist governments limited many freedoms of their citizens, including the liberty to freely leave the country. The U.S. policy during

(Opposite page) Haitian refugees, who fled poverty and in some cases political oppression, await word of their fate inside a compound established at the U.S. Navy base in Guantanamo Bay, Cuba.

the cold war was to provide refuge for people who were able to escape from communist countries. The American leaders believed that communism was wrong and that it led to the formation of a totalitarian government that oppressed the people. President Harry Truman said in 1952:

> The countries of Eastern Europe have fallen under the Communist yoke—they are silenced, fenced off by barbed wire and minefields—no one passes their borders but at the risk of his life. We do not need to be protected against immigrants from these countries—on the contrary we want to stretch out a helping hand, to save those who have managed to flee into Western Europe, to succor those who are brave enough to escape from barbarism, to welcome and restore them against the day when their countries will, as we hope, be free again.

The U.S. refugee policy has always been based on foreign policy, whose primary goal has often been to stop communism. When the Soviet Union sent in tanks to stop citizen protests in Hungary in 1956, the United States decided to accept more than 30,000 refugees who fled from communist control. When Fidel Castro helped engineer the communist takeover of Cuba in 1959, the United States welcomed more than 130,000 refugees.

A Hungarian refugee family arrives in New York in the 1950s.

When the U.S. military forces pulled out of Vietnam in 1973, the communist North Vietnamese took over the south, and the United States accepted nearly 140,000 South Vietnamese refugees.

When refugees arrive in the United States, their adjustment to the culture is relatively similar to the process immigrants undergo, but refugees must follow a very different path in order to be admitted into the country.

Who is a refugee?

The United States accepted only 142,000 of an estimated 1 million refugees who wanted to be admitted in 1992. As part of foreign policy, the president and the State Department determine how many refugees the country should admit each year and from which countries it will accept refugees. Refugees may be admitted because they fall within a preestablished category or because their individual circumstances qualify them as refugees.

The categories established for 1992 followed traditional foreign policy concerns, and refugees who are fleeing from communist governments continued to be preferred. The United States reserved sixty-three thousand spaces for refugees from the former Soviet Union in 1992. The communist Soviet Union outlawed most religious activities, and members of religious groups are still oppressed in the former Soviet republics. Most Soviet refugees are members of religious groups such as Jews and Christians, who are culturally persecuted. For example, Valentin and his family are Soviet refugees who left because Christians were treated poorly in their native country. Valentin said:

> Even the teachers would tease us about being Christians. I used to have to sit in class while the teacher taught us that Christians are bad people.

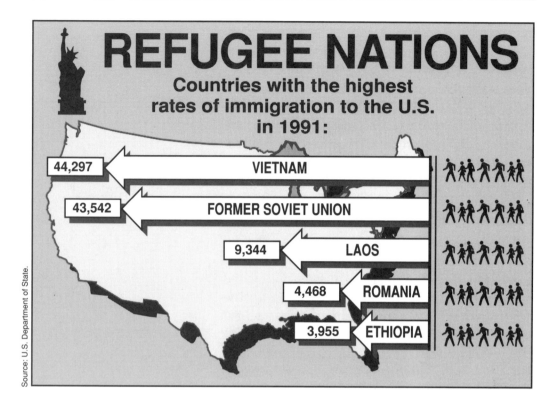

REFUGEE NATIONS
Countries with the highest rates of immigration to the U.S. in 1991:

VIETNAM	44,297
FORMER SOVIET UNION	43,542
LAOS	9,344
ROMANIA	4,468
ETHIOPIA	3,955

Source: U.S. Department of State.

And Christian people can't go to college in my country because the colleges don't want Christians there. Many Christian people tried to get into college in my city, but they couldn't.

Almost all the refugee categories in the United States are based on helping people oppressed by communism. The State Department reserved fifty-two thousand spaces for East Asian refugees who are endangered by the communist governments of South Vietnam, Cambodia, and Laos. Other categories based on freeing people from communism allowed refugees to come from Romania, Poland, Cuba, Ethiopia, and Afghanistan. Additionally, the category for Iranian refugees allowed people to escape the totalitarian religious state created by the Ayatollah Khomeini.

Most refugees that come to the United States are admitted because they fit one of the specific categories established by the State Department. Other refugees are admitted based on individual circumstances. The United States helps refugees who are admitted by category to relocate. Refugees who are not approved in advance, however, often arrive in the United States as illegal aliens and then ask for political asylum. Asylum seekers in the United States have the right to a hearing to explain why it is dangerous to return to their native country. Their immigration status, whether legal or illegal, is not relevant.

Proving persecution

The immigration judge determines whether refugees should be granted political asylum based on the definition provided by the 1980 Refugee Act. A refugee is a person who is unable or unwilling to return to his or her native country because of "persecution, or a well-founded fear of persecution, based on his or her race, religion, nationality, political opinion, or membership in a particular social group." Persecution means to harass, injure, afflict, or oppress a person and specifically, to cause a person to suffer or to be put to death because of his or her beliefs.

Refugees must prove, by showing evidence, that they would be in danger if they were to return to their native country. The INS application instructs refugees to provide this evidence through supporting documents. In addition to their own statements detailing their reasons for seeking refuge, applicants frequently use magazine and newspaper articles, sworn statements from witnesses or experts, personal journals, books, photographs, and official documents to support their case.

For example, a newspaper article may describe the actions of a death squad trying to kill members of a certain group. Other evidence, such as

Cubans seeking asylum in the United States wave to onlookers as they await processing in Florida in 1980.

membership cards, birth records, or the alien's own testimony, may document the alien's membership in the persecuted group. Asylum seekers present their evidence to an immigration judge who decides if they meet the definition of a refugee to the United States.

Critical considerations

The United States limits its refugee policy to cover only those people who are persecuted in their native land. But some critics believe that these policies let some refugees in who are not personally persecuted and keep out others who are persecuted. Some citizens are also concerned about the millions of refugees worldwide who have a real need for a new homeland but are not welcomed here because they are not persecuted and do not fit into any of the established categories.

The refugee categories established each year by the State Department represent large groups of people that the United States considers to be persecuted by their government. Critics complain that this allows people to enter as refugees for any number of reasons. For example, the United States first recognized Cubans as refugees when they fled the new communist regime in large numbers in 1960. A second wave of Cubans sought political asylum in 1980.

The United States quickly recognized these Cubans as a refugee category. President Jimmy Carter welcomed the refugees and said, "We'll continue to provide an open heart and open our minds to refugees seeking freedom from Communist domination and from the economic deprivation brought about by Fidel Castro and his government." More than 120,000 Cuban refugees arrived in the United States in the following six months.

But critics point out that not every individual

within a refugee category is personally persecuted. Augustin, for example, was a Cuban
refugee who worked as a master ship plumber.
He had once served a brief jail sentence for
breaking Cuban laws, but he was not under
surveillance, tortured, or threatened with death.
His country valued his contribution at the ship-
yards, but Augustin wanted to leave anyway.

"I made money," said Augustin. "Oh, yes.
There is no doubt of that. But what can you buy
in Cuba? What can you spend money on? There
is no way for young people to enjoy life in Cuba,
no dancing, no good times. I felt like I was suffo-
cating. Always I felt that way."

Friends and foes

Some critics, such as Charles Creely, professor
of international migration at Georgetown University in Washington, D.C., believe that by basing
refugee admission primarily on categories, the
United States accepts refugees because it dislikes
a particular government and leaves out many
truly persecuted people whose lives are at risk.
Creely said:

> The U.S. uses refugees as a tool of its foreign pol-
> icy. It's just easier to get refugee status if you're
> fleeing a Communist country or a non-Communist
> country with which the U.S. has particularly bad
> relations, such as Iran.

The United States does closely limit which
refugees and how many are allowed to enter as a
matter of foreign policy. Accepting refugees can
insult the country they are fleeing. When the
United States accepts a person as a political
refugee, it is also openly criticizing the native
country, accusing it of violating the basic human
rights of its people. If the United States believes
someone cannot return to their country without
being killed, for example, then the United States

is accusing that country's government of either killing its citizens or failing to protect them. These are serious charges for one country to make against another.

The United States does not like to grant refugee status to people who come from countries with which the United States has good relations. A person who is from a country considered a friend, or ally, of the United States will find it difficult to receive refugee status. This was the case of refugees from El Salvador during the 1980s.

Death squads in El Salvador target students, members of religious groups, and others, but persecuted Salvadorans are not one of the refugee categories preferred by the United States. The United States supported the government in El Salvador and did not want to upset diplomatic relations by accepting its refugees. Many American citizens were outraged that their government turned its back on these refugees and their stories.

Seeking sanctuary

Many Salvadorans, for example, were tortured or threatened with death before they came to the United States. Ana left El Salvador with her parents because her father, a photojournalist, took pictures of people killed by death squads. Her father used the pictures to help relatives identify the dead people. When the government threatened him, the family fled to the United States.

The Salvadoran refugees were helped by a growing sanctuary movement in the United States. Churches and individuals offered refuge to these newcomers, hiding their location and identity from immigration officials. The American Friends Service Committee was among the leaders of this movement, joined by Lutherans and Catholics and many other denominations that offered sanctuary to refugees not recognized or ad-

Social worker Sarah Martinez fled her native El Salvador after her husband was imprisoned, tortured, and killed by death squads.

mitted by the United States. Most of these refugees were from El Salvador, but they also came from other war-torn areas of Central America, including Nicaragua and Guatemala.

People involved in the sanctuary movement believed that refugees from countries such as El Salvador were as worthy of asylum in the United States as refugees from the Soviet Union or Vietnam. The sanctuary movement's willingness to defy immigration laws helped to draw attention to the plight of these refugees. Eventually, the United States decided to hear their cases and grant asylum on an individual basis.

More than 73,000 people applied for political asylum in 1990, but the countries from which most people applied were not the countries with the most successful applications. More than 22,000 Salvadorans, 18,000 Nicaraguans, and 12,000 Guatemalans applied for asylum. This represented 72 percent of all political asylum applications. But only 5,672 people were granted asylum, among them 2,277 Nicaraguans and 679 Chinese. Chinese asylum requests and approvals became much more common after the Tiananmen Square massacre in June 1989.

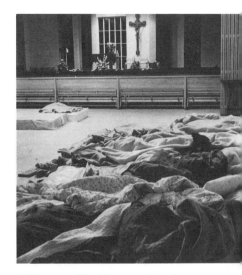

A Tacoma, Washington, church provides sanctuary for a Salvadoran family. Church members viewed the family as refugees; the government viewed the family as illegal aliens.

Fleeing poverty

Some people are excluded by the U.S. refugee policy. The United States does not admit economic refugees or refugees from violent conditions, such as war, who are not individually persecuted. Economic refugees are people whose native land is so poor that their lives are at risk from chronic unemployment, extended droughts, and lack of food. The United States does not accept these economic refugees.

Raymond is typical of many economic refugees. He is from Haiti, one of the most densely populated and least developed countries

A Haitian slum near the port city of Port-au-Prince. Much of the country's population lives in poverty, with houses often lacking electricity and plumbing.

in the Western Hemisphere. Living conditions, including access to jobs, food, and medical care, are so poor that the average Haitian lives to about the age of fifty. Raymond has a family of twelve children in Haiti. He had less than two acres of land to farm, and his family was constantly hungry. He decided to go to the United States to find a job:

> And so I am here in Florida, and I am sending money back, and my wife has written me that our children are healthier than they have ever been. I pray every day that an immigration officer will not come and take me to a detention center. I have no green card, no permit to work. But I must work or my children will die.

Economic refugees do not meet the definition of a refugee and are not part of an established refugee category. Duke Austin, who works at the INS, explained that the same basic human issues are not at stake with economic refugees. "There is a big difference," Austin said, "between fearing for your life and wanting to come here just because you live in poverty and can't find work."

Refugee camps

Many people believe the United States should accept economic refugees because they are similar to many immigrant groups in the country's past. The millions of Irish who escaped the potato famine in the 1840s, for example, were economic refugees. In the last two decades, 20 percent of Jamaica's population has immigrated to the United States, primarily to escape the poor economic conditions of that country. Many believe that economic refugees should be admitted, if not as refugees, then as regular immigrants.

Many refugees leave to escape violent conditions in their homeland, often caused by civil war, war with other countries, and military-controlled governments. These refugees are also ex-

cluded because they are not individually persecuted. The United Nations estimates that more than sixteen million people in the world are refugees. They live in refugee camps around the globe, where barbed wire, boredom, and overcrowded shelters are common features of the generally poor living conditions.

Refugee camps are near the native country in most cases. Refugees usually have to leave their homes quickly, with little planning or preparation. Most must leave behind money and property and are lucky to escape with their lives. They do not usually have the resources to travel far. Many refugee camps, in fact, are near the border of the native country. Sometimes, refugee camps are formed on nearby island nations, such as the Vietnamese camps organized in Malaysia or the Haitian camp at the U.S. Navy base in Guantanamo Bay, Cuba.

Sending people home

Most of these sixteen million refugees will remain in camps until it is safe for them to return to their homes. The United States may welcome only a small percentage of the world's refugees,

Vietnamese refugees wade ashore in Malaysia. There, they live in refugee camps until the Malaysian government decides whether to grant asylum or send them home.

but it helps provide funding for the International Red Cross and the United Nations, which provide temporary shelters, food, clothing, and medical care for refugees in these camps. The United States also helps refugees diplomatically, often negotiating with the native country to help end the violence that caused the refugees to flee.

One goal of U.S. refugee policy is repatriation, which means to permanently resettle refugees back in their country of origin. For most of the world's refugees, the conditions necessary for repatriation have not been met. The violence or terror that caused the refugees to leave in the first place must be stopped before it is safe for these people to go back. Conditions in Cambodia, Angola, and Ethiopia, however, had improved so that more than three million refugees could return home in 1992.

For most refugees, returning home is not possible and is not a solution to their problem. Many refugees will live in temporary refugee camps for years, especially if they are not accepted into the United States. Malaysian refugee camps have held Vietnamese asylum seekers since 1975. The United States became more selective about which Vietnamese refugees it accepted in the 1990s, and those rejected have nowhere else to live. The Malaysians have argued for forced, or involuntary, repatriation, which means sending the refugees back to Vietnam against their will. The United States opposes forced repatriation.

Haitians at sea

Repatriation is also an issue with the Haitian refugees. Haiti was governed for many years by dictator Jean-Claude Duvalier. Duvalier used a secret police force that terrorized the population and created fear among the citizens to promote his power. Haitians revolted against Duvalier in

Haitians arrive at the Guantanamo Bay refugee camp. Many were sent directly back to Haiti, prompting protest from refugee organizations and other groups.

HAITIAN IMMIGRATION

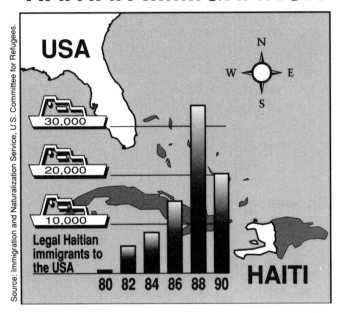

Source: Immigration and Naturalization Service, U.S. Committee for Refugees.

1986 and disbanded the secret police force. But the Haitian government that replaced Duvalier was unstable and was alternately controlled by the military and civilians. The United States and the Organization of American States helped to monitor free elections in Haiti in 1990, and Jean-Bertrand Aristide was elected president. Seven months later, though, this democratic government was overthrown by a military coup. The United States tried to pressure the coup leaders into giving up power by placing an economic embargo on Haiti. While the embargo had support from many, including Aristide, it squeezed an already impoverished nation even further. In hopes of escaping the dire conditions, and in some cases, political recrimination, many Haitians boarded leaky boats for the United States. An unknown number of Haitian refugees died at sea on their way to south Florida. Because no country in the Caribbean or nearby was willing to accept the large number of fleeing Haitians, the United States positioned Coast Guard cutters twelve miles away from Haiti's shores. The Coast Guard intercepted boatloads of Haitians and returned them to their country.

This created a public outcry. Many people called these actions forced repatriation, which the American government opposed when Malaysia tried to send back boatloads of Vietnamese refugees. But the United States insists repatriation of Haitians is different.

International agreements require a country to take responsibility only for refugees inside its borders. The Vietnamese were housed in Malaysian refugee camps when the Malaysian government tried to send them away. The Haitians, on the other hand, were on open seas and so were not the responsibility of the U.S. government, American officials said.

For these reasons, the State Department viewed the return of Haitians as a humanitarian act. The primary purpose, officials said, was to save the lives of Haitians attempting to leave in boats that were not seaworthy.

A continuing concern

The State Department is concerned that every attempt it makes to provide assistance for Haitians encourages additional refugees. When Haitians first arrived by the tens of thousands during the 1980s, the Coast Guard picked up the refugees traveling in boats that were not seaworthy and took them to Florida, but then the numbers of refugees just increased. So, the United States established a refugee camp for the Haitians at the naval base on Guantanamo Bay in Cuba. By May 1992, with Haitian refugees exiting at the rate of more than ten thousand a month, Guantanamo had surpassed its capacity.

Haitian soldiers patrol the streets of Port-au-Prince just days before the 1990 presidential election. Seven months later, the new president was overthrown and thousands of Haitians tried to flee.

President George Bush ordered the Coast Guard to return all Haitian refugees on the sea back to Haiti on May 24, 1992. The refugees are met on the dock by officers of the U.S. embassy and are advised about how to apply for asylum at the American embassy in Haiti. The United States began processing refugee applications in Port-au-Prince, Haiti, in February 1992. In the first month alone, there were several thousand applications. The State Department plans to admit Haitian refugees who have been politically persecuted, such as those who "hold or held leadership positions in political or religious organizations at the national or local level, have held sensitive positions in the Aristide Government, or are prominent in fields that may be targets of pressure."

Haitian refugees will likely be a continuing concern for the United States, at least until a democratic government is restored in Haiti and the embargo is lifted. While the State Department continues working to restore the Aristide government, it also tries to establish the best policy it can for the refugees and believes that returning them to Haiti is the safest, most humanitarian action it can take. In the first week the United States started returning Haitian refugees directly back to Haiti, the Coast Guard pickups dropped from several thousand a week to a few dozen. If this continues, it means Haitian refugees will be much less likely to die at sea. But many Haitians will continue to seek refuge in the United States because the severity of living conditions in Haiti will force them out.

Haitians who sought refuge in the United States arrive back in Haiti after the U.S. Supreme Court ruled that repatriation could continue.

5

Open or Closed Borders

THE UNITED STATES opens its borders to new people. Some countries have closed borders and do not accept immigrants, and a few do not even accept visitors. Whether a country is considered to have open or closed borders depends on how freely the government lets in other people or how strictly it keeps them out. Even a country with relatively open borders, such as the United States, closes those borders to some people in some way.

A country may allow or not allow immigration for many reasons. The United States, for example, tends to want immigration partly because of its history as a nation of immigrants. Japan, on the other hand, generally does not allow immigration, believing it would be culturally disruptive to have foreigners within its society. France admits few permanent immigrants but allows many foreigners to live and work there.

Most people in the United States do not want either completely open or completely closed borders. Completely open borders would allow unlimited immigration. Anyone in the world would be allowed to move to the United States. Some Americans fear the country would lose its identity

(Opposite page) The Statue of Liberty has served for more than one hundred years as a symbol of American freedom and opportunity. It has had special meaning for the thousands of immigrants who have passed by it as they approached American shores.

if immigration were completely open. Some citizens fear that uncontrolled borders would allow in so many people that the United States could become an overcrowded, unattractive place to live.

Completely closed borders would stop all immigration to the country. Closed borders would keep out the foreign-born family members of citizens who want to join their husbands, wives, sons, daughters, mothers, and fathers. Closed borders would keep out scientists, nurses, and field workers who help raise the standard of living in the United States. Closed borders would keep out a continual flow of people and their ideas, upon which many citizens believe American culture is built.

Absolutely open or closed borders are extremes, and both options are supported by relatively few Americans. Most citizens agree that the government should let in some but not all of the immigrants who would like to come to the United States. People still disagree, though, about the number of immigrants and which immigrants should be given priority consideration.

Limiting immigration

The United States has historically tried to admit people from all over the globe, but it has also closed its doors at various times to certain immigrants. Some of the first limits on immigration were designed to keep out people who came from China, Japan, Poland, Greece, and Italy. Many citizens believed these immigrants, who brought unfamiliar religions, foods, and customs with them, threatened to overwhelm American culture. The United States tried to protect its national identity by limiting immigration. Quotas passed in 1925 limited how many immigrants could come from any one country and also specified which countries were allowed to send immi-

'GEE, I'M SORRY, THE NEW TRIBAL GUEST WORKER QUOTAS ARE FILLED. WHY DON'T YOU TRY AGAIN NEXT YEAR!'

grants. The quotas favored immigrants from northern and western Europe and made it nearly impossible for immigrants to come from countries in Asia or Africa. Those immigrants who were allowed to come to the United States provided greatly needed labor for the growing economy. Most advocates of open immigration at the time believed immigrant labor was an essential part of American prosperity.

The U.S. immigration policy changed dramatically in the 1960s. Critics attacked the quota system as racist. Author Julian Simon said, "The notion of wanting to keep out immigrants in order to keep our institutions and our values is pure prejudice." Many believed the nation of immigrants should offer a more fair, more open immi-

President Lyndon Johnson signs the 1965 immigration law which gave priority to reunifying families.

gration policy. Congress responded with the 1965 Immigration Act.

The new law based admission on family reunification rather than the immigrant's country of origin. Family reunification helps families that are separated join each other again. The law established a category system that gave immigration preference to immediate family members of U.S. citizens. Other preference categories admitted the siblings and married children of citizens as well as the immediate family and spouses of permanent residents. The 1965 law also permitted employment-based immigration, reserving 10 percent of the spaces for people who had job skills needed in the United States.

Two primary reasons are behind this strong preference for family reunification. One is humanitarian concern. Family members should be able to live near each other if they choose, the government believes, and immediate family members of U.S. citizens are therefore given the highest preference for immigrating. The other reason for preferring family reunification is that many experts believe immigrants are more successful and adapt better to American culture when they are sponsored by a family member who will show them the way things are done in the United States and will financially support them until they are able to support themselves.

Too many or too few?

Several years after the 1965 law went into effect, some citizens became concerned about the results it produced. Historically, immigration to the United States came mostly from Europe, but with the quotas removed, immigration came mostly from Asia and Latin America. The preference for family reunification severely limited immigrants with needed labor skills or the means to start their own business.

These concerns were addressed when Congress revised the immigration laws in 1990. Family-sponsored immigrants still have more than half of the available spaces at 480,000, but Congress also reserved 140,000 slots for employment-based immigration. The 1990 law opened total immigration to 675,000 newcomers each year. The United States began the twentieth century with its first limits on immigration, and although immigration has remained limited, the major revisions of the law have today opened the doors to more immigrants from more countries.

Citizens still differ over whether the borders should be more open or closed. Many believe that the United States lets in too many immigrants, and some believe the country should allow in more. These citizens may believe that immigrants compete for jobs and take work away from Americans. They may believe that the country needs immigrant labor skills to compete internationally, especially in the sciences. Some people are concerned that government services, the environment, and the country's natural resources cannot support a large population. Citizens also become concerned about maintaining the American culture and often feel threatened when immigrants arrive from drastically different cultures. Many Americans believe that immigration policy should be changed to meet the needs of Americans, rather than the needs of immigrants.

Countries of origin

Immigration to the United States has not been based on country of origin since 1965, but some citizens believe this should be a more important consideration. Some citizens want to limit immigration so that most of the immigrants have European origins. The majority of Americans are of European origin. More than 50 percent of the American people reported in the 1990 census that they are at least partly of German origin. White people make up about 80 percent of the total U.S.

WOULD YOU WANT TO LIVE IN A HOUSE WITHOUT DOORS?

population. Some citizens believe these are—and should remain—the characteristics that define American society.

Europe is no longer the dominant source of immigrants coming to America, however. Barely nineteen thousand immigrants arrived from England, Scotland, Wales, and Northern Ireland in 1990. All of northern and western Europe sent less than 3 percent of total 1990 immigration. Instead, most immigrants—more than 80 percent in 1990—were from Asia and Latin America. Most of these newcomers do not speak English when they arrive. A 1992 poll by the *Los Angeles Times* found that of 750 Koreans, 47 percent reported they spoke English not at all or not well. Only 14 percent reported that they used only English or mostly English in their daily life, and 53 percent said they used mostly Korean or only Korean. Many Americans believe that by limiting immigration primarily to Europeans, the newcomers will be more like Americans in their culture, political thinking, and language.

Creating new spaces

Immigration based on family reunification favors immigrants from countries that have recently sent large numbers of immigrants to the United States. For example, immigrants from Mexico, which has recently sent large numbers of its citizens, are much more likely to have close family members living in the United States than are potential immigrants from Nepal, which has sent very few immigrants. Since 1965, most immigrants have arrived from Asia and Latin America, so new family-based immigrants from those areas are more likely to be accepted than are newcomers from England, Scotland, Ireland, Norway, or Germany who do not have U.S. relatives—even though these European countries once dominated

American immigration.

Congress responded to these concerns in a 1990 immigration law. Congress reserved fifty-five thousand spaces each year from 1990 to 1993 for immigrants from thirty-four countries who found it difficult to immigrate under the family reunification plan. Presumably, these new immigrants from Europe will increase the American family ties of more Europeans and therefore increase European immigration under family re-unification.

Many critics also believe that immigration should be based more on employment than on family reunification. Immigrants make important contributions to the economy, especially to science and technology. Employment-based immigration has always been encouraged by U.S. policy, but it made up only a small percentage of total immigration under the 1965 law. Many of these workers are nurses and other medical professionals, more than three thousand of which are recruited from the Philippines each year. Critics argued that per-

GIVE ME YOUR SCIENTISTS, YOUR DOCTORS, YOUR TEACHERS, BUT KEEP YOUR OTHER EXPORTS TO YOURSELVES

ROTHCO

mission to move to the United States is so difficult for many potential immigrants, however, that it keeps out people who would benefit the American economy. Immigration attorney Carl Shusterman said, "U.S. immigration laws have been so eccentric and arbitrary that, it is said, even Albert Einstein, were he alive today, would have a difficult time qualifying for a green card."

Professionals

Many citizens agreed with Shusterman, believing that the United States was not recruiting enough professional talent among its immigrants. Employers wishing to legally hire a foreign-born worker first had to receive a labor certification by proving that "no U.S. employee is ready, willing, and able to perform a certain job for which a qualified foreign-born worker is available." The certification process could take from six months to several years. Employment-based immigration policies imposed the same requirements for agricultural field workers or domestic laborers as it did for chemists and nuclear scientists. And many critics, including Shusterman, argued the difference was important enough to change the law:

> Scientists are not like assembly-line workers. The contributions of foreign-born scientists in aiding medical research or in making a discovery that assists in the development of a new technology, are inestimable. One foreign-born scientist recently obtained a patent for his U.S. employer for a process to produce a drug that has enhanced the lives of tens of thousands of dialysis patients (and has, incidentally, created employment for more than 1,000 Americans). Other examples of the dramatic contribution of foreign-born scientists—from the Manhattan Project to the moon landing—abound.

American businesses successfully urged the government to increase employment-based immigration. Congress included this goal in the 1990 law, which nearly tripled spaces reserved for these immigrants, raising the limits from 54,000 to 140,000 annually, and created several categories of employment-based immigration. A new priority category allows scientists with demonstrated extraordinary ability to immigrate without labor certification. These spaces are limited to scientists who have established an international reputation for their work.

The next preference category is for scientists of exceptional ability and with advanced academic degrees. Applicants from this category must still supply a labor certification before they get permission to immigrate. The 1990 law reserves spaces in its third employment-based category for workers who have only a bachelor's degree and other skilled and unskilled workers, all of whom must also have labor certification before they immigrate.

Benefits and burdens

Congress also reserved ten thousand immigration spaces under the 1990 law to encourage entrepreneurs to immigrate. The law allows businesspeople and their families to immigrate if they invest one million dollars in an American business that creates at least ten new jobs. The investment requirement can be lowered to half a million dollars if the business is in a rural area or located in certain areas with high unemployment.

Some existing American businesses tried to take advantage of this new category and placed ads in foreign publications, such as the Hong Kong edition of the *Wall Street Journal*, seeking investors in their business. Many businesspeople in Hong Kong are trying to leave before the country comes under control of communist China in 1997. One of the earliest investors under this program was twenty-two-year-old Wu Wen-shuo,

Austrian immigrant Fred Rossmeissl is willing to invest money in a plastics business so he can remain in America.

who borrowed more than one million dollars from his family to buy a gas station and a car wash in Chula Vista, California. Wu Wen-shuo was enrolled in the medical school at the University of California, Los Angeles, when the law went into effect, and the law made it possible for him to stay in the United States when he graduated.

The 1990 law increased the total number of immigrants from the 1965 limit of 270,000 to 675,000 each year. Some people, including former President George Bush and Gene McNary, head of the Immigration and Naturalization Service, believe that the United States can absorb more than one million immigrants a year. In fact, some observers believe the American economy and culture could easily absorb several million immigrants annually. Others, such as Richard Lamm, former governor of Colorado, strongly disagree. Lamm, for example, argues that the United States has limited resources that cannot support additional people.

Some Americans, including former Colorado governor Richard Lamm (above), believe the United States admits too many new immigrants. Crowded unemployment offices, such as the one below, fuel the argument that immigration should be limited as long as citizens are without jobs.

American jobs are a big concern for people who want to keep immigration limits relatively low. Many citizens believe that admitting large numbers of immigrants hurts American workers by taking away jobs that could go to native-born people and by allowing working conditions to deteriorate. The effect of immigration on the American economy is difficult to measure. Some people argue that a limited number of jobs is available each year and if the country allows in several hundred thousand immigrants, then more people will compete for these limited jobs. Many citizens feel that immigration should remain limited as long as the United States has unemployment.

The cost of government services causes many taxpayers to want to limit immigration. Large populations, whether they are native-born or immigrants, use huge amounts of government services. Large populations drive more cars, so roads wear down quicker and cost more to be maintained and repaired. Police and fire protection services require more officers for more people. Bigger populations also create more trash, and the government must spend more money collecting and disposing of the community's garbage. Larger populations generally force increases in all areas of government services.

Financial woes

Many government services are already in crisis. American schools, police forces, medical facilities, and landfills are already overburdened by a large population. Increasing that population, through immigration or other means, could severely limit the government's ability to meet basic needs in an acceptable manner. The federal government does reimburse the state for refugee costs and makes some allowances for estimated populations of illegal aliens, but even when the federal government attempts to pay back some of these costs, the state and local governments must bear the burden of these costs. In some cases, such as in Los Angeles, the costs are estimated to be considerably higher than the amount reimbursed or collected in taxes or user fees.

Public school systems are especially burdened by large and rapid increases in population. South Florida, for example, faced a growing population as refugees, immigrants, and illegal aliens arrived in the area throughout the 1980s and 1990s. The Dade County schools literally could not construct school buildings fast enough to keep up with the demand for space. The school system had to hire more teachers, buy more buses, and order more textbooks. Growing populations place the same kind of pressure on hospitals trying to keep down the cost of medical care, police departments trying to reduce crime, and fire departments that must be able to respond promptly to emergency calls.

Many citizens are upset that newcomers are allowed to receive welfare payments, which some

citizens do not believe should be available even for the native-born. Immigrants are eligible on the same basis as citizens to receive food stamps, Medicaid, and support from Aid to Families with Dependent Children. After an immigrant has worked long enough in the United States, he or she also becomes eligible for unemployment benefits and Social Security income, which includes Medicare and disability benefits.

Peter Brimelow, an editor at *Forbes* magazine, is among those who believe immigrants should not receive welfare payments. Brimelow wrote:

> Earlier waves of immigrants were basically free to succeed or fail. And many failed: as much as a third of the 1880-1920 immigrants returned to their native lands. But with the current wave, public policy interposes itself, with the usual debatable results.

Brimelow and many others believe that finding a job that can support one's self and one's family is the risk that immigrants take when they come to the United States. Historically, all immigrants have taken this risk. Brimelow believes that providing welfare assistance unfairly reduces the risks of immigration at a cost paid by taxpayers.

However, immigrants are taxpayers. Immigrants pay sales, property, and income taxes as well as Social Security taxes, user fees, and license costs. Increasing the population through immigration can actually increase the amount of taxes collected and, therefore, increase the amount of money available to pay for government services. And as immigrants assimilate into the culture, some will be elected to school boards, serve as hospital directors, and become contributing members of this society. They will help to build and pay for these government services.

An open door

The government responds to citizens' concerns about immigration by selecting who is allowed to immigrate. Family-based immigration is supposed to relieve immigrant dependence on the government because the family agrees to sponsor the newcomer, paying for any expenses until the immigrant is established. Employment-based immigration is also supposed to reduce the chance that immigrants will receive welfare payments because they have a job waiting when they get to the United States.

Whether they are concerned about government costs, protecting American jobs, or preserving the European-based culture, most Americans believe that it is important to limit immigration. In fact, almost 70 percent of people in the United States believe that the country should accept fewer total immigrants each year. The majority of Americans believe current immigration policy opens the door too widely.

6

Salad Bowl or Melting Pot

THE UNITED STATES has often been described as a social experiment. Immigrants formed this nation by choosing to be similar to one another and coming together to form a common culture. As one observer noted, Americans

> do not subscribe to a common religious or racial heritage; instead, our cultural ideals are inclusionary: They accommodate everyone who will share the commitment to democracy, toleration, mobility, and the rule of law.

Part of the American social experiment was immigration. The United States opened its doors to people from all over the world. New immigrants were expected to adopt American ways, or Americanize, when they arrived. The United States absorbed immigrants from all classes of people who arrived from countries throughout Europe. The United States was called a melting pot because as immigrants became part of American society, their old ways and the various cultures mingled together until the different parts had become an integrated whole.

The melting pot theory claims that American culture is constantly being formed and reformed as more people are added to it. It is assumed that

(Opposite page) A crowd gathers for a New York City parade, revealing the diversity of America.

An 1880 drawing depicts America giving an enthusiastic welcome to immigrants fleeing war and distress.

every immigrant can be absorbed by the culture and contribute to it. The metaphor of the melting pot has been used to explain the process that immigrants undergo as they adjust to American culture and as American culture adjusts to them. But the melting pot also describes what early Americans wanted—a culture in which new and diverse members were more alike than different. Americans expected immigrants to change.

Immigrants who have changed and adopted American culture are considered to be assimilated. Assimilation is the process through which immigrants and other newcomers are absorbed into the culture. Both the newcomer and the culture may change during this process. For example, the immigrant may learn English, while the immigrant's knowledge of how to use a wok to stir-fry foods becomes part of the culture. Assimilation is an important part of the melting pot view of America. Newcomers had to assimilate to "melt" into the culture.

The American melting pot contains cultural influences from every immigrant group that has entered the United States. Other countries have also been tremendously influenced by immigration. Almost every country in Europe, for example, has cultural influences that date back to a time of immigration or conquest. In England, waves of Roman, Saxon, Viking, and Norman immigration permanently affected the modern English language, and their influence can also be seen today in such things as the names of England's cities and towns. But American immigration is unique. Not only did the United States encourage immigration, but it accepted a more diverse group of people over a shorter amount of time and still expected all of them to assimilate.

A nation of immigrants

The United States is a nation of immigrants, but it is a nation of immigrants that adapted to the particular ideals, values, and cultural traits that define an American. Immigrants and native-born citizens in the United States may be allowed to choose their own religion, criticize the government, and develop individual manners and values, but as a whole, Americans want residents to speak English, to believe in and adhere to constitutional democracy and freedoms, and to share the values and practices that are believed to have advanced Western civilization. Americans want the melting pot to change newcomers more than the newcomers change the melting pot.

The nineteenth-century immigrants from southern and eastern Europe caused many people to question the melting pot idea. These immigrants were culturally and ethnically different from most of the people already in the United States. Many critics feared that the differences

Nineteenth-century Americans worried that southern and eastern European immigrants such as this Hungarian family would not be able to "melt" into society.

were so great, that the new immigrants would not be able to adjust to the United States and the country would not be able to merge them into its culture. But this was not a new concern.

Benjamin Franklin, for example, worried about the German influence in Pennsylvania before the Revolution. In 1751, Franklin asked, "Why should Pennsylvania, founded by the English, become a Colony of *Aliens*, who will shortly be so numerous as to Germanize us instead of our Anglifying them?"

The same fears were expressed about Chinese immigrants in California during the nineteenth century. Many of these immigrants retained their native language, religion, and other cultural traits. The fear that these immigrants would threaten the American social experiment was so great that the United States established immigration laws and a quota system to make sure that most new immigrants arrived from northern and western Europe.

The melting pot survived the apparent threat of the diverse immigrant groups of the late 1800s. In fact, by the mid-1960s, many people believed the melting pot had proved itself by assimilating the children of those immigrants. Many citizens believed that the melting pot was capable of absorbing diverse immigrants if they arrived in small enough numbers. Americans limit immigration even today to try to preserve American culture.

The American mosaic

The melting pot idea may have been a good description of the United States, but by the 1970s many people believed that the description should be changed to include more individual and group differences. Some people suggested that instead of a melting pot, the United States should try to be more like a salad bowl in which the various parts are still recognizable but complement each other.

Some social scientists promoted the notion of an American salad bowl with research suggesting that the melting pot had not completely melted after all. For example, historian Reed Ueda said:

> The melting pot as a social and cultural reality in history was never Anglo-conformist or homogeneous. . . . Groups changed and merged like the images of a kaleidoscope, with astounding and unpredictable patterns of diversity that yet cohered into a unity. Moreover, many features of group life were left unmelted and unfused.

Some sociologists said the United States was more accurately described as a core culture that is British-American. That core culture acts as a host society that can tolerate a large amount of individual and group diversity but also demands its newcomers and ethnic minorities to fit into the core culture in basic ways. These newcomers must, for example, speak English, participate in the economy, and obey the laws.

Some people suggest that a salad bowl, with all its diverse ingredients and distinct flavors, is a more fitting description of American society than the melting pot.

A salad bowl

Other social scientists described the United States as a pluralistic society. Pluralism is the existence of many different subcultures within the society. The pluralistic description is closest to the salad bowl idea. The subcultures may be created by people of different national heritage, religion, race, age, political alliance, or other characteristics. Members of each of these subcultures may pursue a life-style different from the others, but they share a government and an economy through which they come together to address common needs and goals.

This notion of pluralism is demonstrated in a report by the LA 2000 Committee, which works on plans for the future of Los Angeles. The committee described Los Angeles as becoming less like a melting pot and more like a salad bowl:

> Think of Los Angeles as a mosaic with every color distinct, vibrant and essential to the whole. Native American, Mexican, African-American, Japanese, Israeli, Chinese, Tongan, Indian, German, Irish, Armenian, Ethiopian, Swedish, Korean, Samoan, Guatemalan, Russian, Arab, Persian, French, Cuban, Italian, Fijian, Australian, Honduran, Scottish, Hungarian, Danish, Malaysian, Filipino, English, Turkish are just some of the more than 100 cultural and ethnic backgrounds that exist together in Los Angeles. Each of these groups makes its own special contribution to the rich mix that is creating a new heritage for the metropolitan area. Each brings its own ethos, arts, ideas, and skills to a community that welcomes and encourages diversity and grows stronger by taking the best from it. They respect each other as mutual partners.

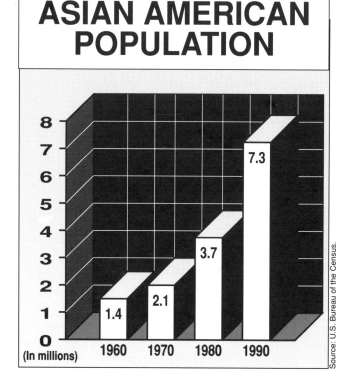

ASIAN AMERICAN POPULATION

8
7
6
5
4
3
2
1
0
(In millions)

7.3
3.7
2.1
1.4

1960 1970 1980 1990

Source: U.S. Bureau of the Census.

Americans have debated this changing view of themselves since the 1960s. Many citizens believe it is important for the United States to accept new ideas and cultural traits. Author Michael Novak emphasizes this point:

> The really important question is: How capable is America of assimilating the wisdom and the perceptions brought by the immigrants? It's not only up to to the immigrants to assimilate; it's also up to America to change and be changed in order to become more like the immigrants.

But many citizens do not want the United States to change. Many citizens believe in the melting pot idea and believe that newcomers should adopt American ways. For these people, the new immigration created by the 1965 Immigration Act allowed in far too many people who were far too different from existing Americans.

Demographics

The changing demographics of the United States concern many people. Demographics are the characteristics that describe a certain population. The population of the United States is becoming increasingly nonwhite and Spanish-speaking, and it includes rapidly rising numbers of Asians and Latinos. To many people, these immigrants seem less likely to adopt American culture and assimilate than previous immigrants did. Some people believe these changes are causing the United States to become more of a salad bowl, less like a melting pot.

Latinos are increasing in numbers in the United States. Tens of thousands of Latinos enter the country through immigration. Latinos are an important force in the politics and economy where they live, especially in the states of California, Texas, Florida, New York, New Jersey, Arizona, Colorado, and Illinois. Latinos

Eung Wha Kim teaches traditional Korean folk dance in her Los Angeles studio. By retaining traditions such as this, do Americans dilute or enrich their heritage?

are 20 percent of New York City's population. They are the largest minority group, outnumbering African-Americans in Los Angeles, San Francisco, and New York City. Latinos are the second largest minority group in the country after African-Americans. Latinos grew from 4.5 percent of the population in 1970 to 9 percent of the population in 1990.

The many immigrants arriving from Asia and Latin America as well as from other nontraditional areas, such as Africa and the Middle East, are changing the demographics of the United States. This change is more apparent in some regions than it is in others. Scientists predict that by the year 2010, California and Texas will no longer have a white majority. Hawaii already has no majority ethnic group among its whites, African-Americans, Asians, Samoans, and Hawaiian Islanders. Demographer Leon Bouvier projects the United States will be 61 percent white by the year 2020.

Many subcultures

These changing demographics are not just the result of accepting more immigrants from Asia and Latin America. The newcomers are not adjusting to the United States in the same way and at the same rate as previous immigrants did. Instead of merging into a nondistinct mass, individual groups remain recognizable. Sometimes, this may be because large populations of newcomers from the same culture can come together to form a subculture within which they can preserve their heritage. Latinos, for example, are entering the United States in such large numbers—both legally and illegally—that newcomers find it easy to retain their native language because they can provide for most of their needs without using English.

The Spanish-speaking economy of south Florida attracts large populations from throughout Central and South America and the Caribbean. Miami supports a Spanish-language newspaper and several Spanish-language television and radio stations, including the highest-rated radio station in the city. Many hospitals, hotels, dress shops, grocery stores, gasoline stations, and restaurants do business in Spanish. Tourists from Latin America spend more than 1.5 billion dollars each year in Miami and south Florida. Miami is such a focal point for Latin America that in most instances, more airline flights go between any one Latin American city and Miami than between any two Latin American cities. The result is that flying from Managua in Nicaragua to Caracas in Venezuela may be easiest through Miami, and sometimes it is the only way to find a connecting flight.

A vendor sells Spanish-language magazines in Miami. In some neighborhoods and communities Spanish is at least as common as English and sometimes even more so.

Los Angeles is another area of dramatic demographic change. Los Angeles and the state of California have promoted their economic and cultural relationship with the countries of the Pacific Rim, including Mexico, Central America, western South America, Southeast Asia, Japan, China, Korea, and the islands in the Pacific. Immigrants from these areas overwhelmingly choose California as their new home.

One Los Angeles resident explained:

> Twenty-first century Los Angeles will combine the best of every culture that has come here. It will combine Asian family loyalty, Hispanic industriousness, and Anglo-Saxon respect for individual liberty. That's an entirely new package; no culture like that has ever been created before.

Not everyone is pleased with seeing the United States become increasingly more like a salad bowl and less like a melting pot. They worry that American society is uncontrollably changing into something foreign. Most of these people do not question the individual right to expression, but many are concerned that American public values and efficiency are eroded by such diversity.

Accepting diversity

British immigrant Peter Brimelow believes that the American mosaic is being forced on the culture, even though most Americans reject it:

> And asking people if they want their communities to be overwhelmed by weird aliens with dubious habits is a stupid question. . . . But the greater the number of immigrants, and the greater their difference from the American mainstream, the louder and ruder the answer will be.

Other Americans believe Brimelow's position is based on prejudice. Many of the people who prefer the salad bowl idea of American culture believe the United States has changed too much to ever accept the melting pot concept again. They believe the diversity of the salad bowl is more fair and a better reflection or description of reality. Many people are willing to accept diverse immigrants into American society because they believe their society can tolerate the differences. As one citizen said, "We learned to eat pizza—that used to be foreign—and we'll learn to eat Thai food, too. People don't come here to be ethnic forever; they come here to make money. All they need is a little space for a generation or two."

Bilingualism

Regardless of whether the United States should strive to be more like a melting pot or a salad bowl, most American people agree that English must be preserved as the culture's language. The United States is an English-speaking country, and most Americans want it to remain so. English is the language the country uses for legal and governmental communication. English is the language of the American economy.

The United States, however, has one of the largest Spanish-speaking populations in the world. Spanish is the second most common language in the United States. Miami has shown that a Spanish-speaking marketplace can attract millions of dollars each month into its economy. Major corporations are adjusting to the needs of their numerous Spanish-speaking consumers, and a call to a major phone company may result in a message, first in English and then in Spanish, reporting that all lines are currently busy.

Spanish is spoken on the streets and used daily by millions of residents, but most Americans do not believe the country should support a bilingual culture that gives equal weight or importance to two languages. Many people fear that equating Spanish with English will destroy the very essence of how Americans define themselves

Signs in a Los Angeles grocery thank customers in both Spanish and English.

culturally. They believe the English language cannot and should not be lost in the process of assimilation.

Bilingual individuals, people who are able to fluently speak, read, and write two languages, have an advantage in the changing American society. A Kansas City, Missouri, magnet school advertises the benefits of bilingual education, noting that bilingual students are more likely to be successful in school and in the economy. California government officials asserted in the 1980s that in order to prepare students for the future, every student in California public schools, even those whose native language is English, should receive a bilingual education.

On a cultural level, however, bilingualism means that society would give equal importance to two languages. Most Americans believe bilingualism is a divisive force in any culture and promotes separatism. Even among immigrants, most believe that learning and using English is

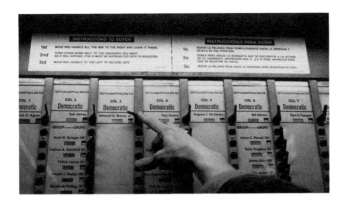

While the majority of Americans speak English, some states provide election ballots and other services in languages other than English.

the only way to truly adapt to life in the United States, and more than 90 percent of U.S.-born Latinos are fluent in English. But in American society, knowledge of Spanish is increasingly important.

Toward a future

Many experts predict that if current immigration rates and population patterns continue in the United States, the country will experience more cultural diversity. Some people believe the United States should fight this trend, but many others believe Americans should prepare for it by learning to better understand the differences in their society. Gene McNary, the director of the INS, explained in 1992 that the United States today is a lot like the United States of yesterday and tomorrow:

> My judgment is that [America is] probably 80 percent melting pot—but around the edges is a mosaic. It may be that that's the way it always will be. I think it takes a generation or two for new groups, new people, to assimilate—become a part of the mainstream. It is likely that even the native-born will face new challenges as all Americans adapt to what the United States was and continues to be—a nation of immigrants.

Glossary

acculturation: The changes that occur in an individual as a result of contact with a new culture.

alien: A foreign-born resident who has not yet become a citizen of the United States.

amnesty: A pardon, or forgiveness, given by the government to a large group of people.

assimilation: The process by which immigrants or other newcomers are absorbed into a culture.

asylum: The protection offered to a refugee by another country's government, including the protection from being returned to his or her native land.

bilingualism: The use of two languages with equal skill.

coyote: Someone who smuggles illegal aliens into the United States.

demographics: The characteristics or descriptions of a group of people, such as the population of a city, region, or country.

deportation: The act of forcing immigrants or other aliens out of the country, usually by sending them back to their native country.

dialect: A form of a language that is used in a particular region and has differences in vocabulary or usage from the primary form of the language.

emigrate: To leave one's native country to live permanently somewhere else. For example, if a native of Thailand moves to the United States, she is an emigrant from Thailand.

ethnic: Regarding the characteristics, values, or other aspects of a particular nationality or other cultural group.

immigrate: To enter a country that is not one's native country to live permanently. For example, if a native of Thailand moves to the United States, she is an immigrant to the United States.

nativism: An attitude or policy that favors the interests of native-born people over those of immigrants.

naturalization: The legal procedure for becoming a citizen.

pluralism: The recognition that many distinct cultural groups exist within one society.

prejudice: An opinion or judgment about a person or a group made prior to meeting or knowing the people.

refuge: The relief, safety, or protection provided by a certain place.

repatriation: To return someone to his or her native country.

restrictionists: People who want to limit immigration.

sanction: A penalty for disobeying rules or laws.

sanctuary: A place that offers safety and protection to someone seeking refuge or asylum.

separatism: A condition of disunity or divisiveness that sets one group apart from the whole.

smuggle: To illegally and secretly bring products or people into or out of a country.

sojourner: Someone who journeys to a new country and intends to stay temporarily and does not intend to become a citizen.

stereotype: An oversimplified definition of a person or group of people, sometimes based on prejudicial opinions.

totalitarian: A form of government in which one person or group of people exercises complete control over all aspects of life in the country.

Organizations to Contact

The following organizations provide services or information about immigration, refugees, and the naturalization process. The addresses and phone numbers are provided so more information can be obtained directly from each organization.

American Friends Service Committee (AFSC)
Mexico/U.S. Border Program
1501 Cherry St.
Philadelphia, PA 19102
(215) 241-7132

AFSC documents INS abuse against immigrants, legal residents, and U.S. citizens. Its programs deal with health, human rights, and economic development. AFSC helps to develop network links among the many organizations working to assist immigrants. It offers several publications about Mexican migration for a small fee.

Church World Service Immigration and Refugee Program
475 Riverside Dr.
New York, NY 10115
(212) 870-3153

Church World Service responds to the plight of refugees, migrants, displaced persons, immigrants, and people seeking asylum. Participant denominations in forty-five offices across the United States cooperate in resettling refugees, assisting immigrants, and providing first asylum services. It supports and participates in the development of national and international policies and programs advocating protection for the uprooted.

The Federation for American Immigration Reform (FAIR)
1666 Connecticut Ave. NW, Suite 400
Washington, DC 20009
(202) 328-7004

FAIR is a public interest organization working to end illegal immigration and set lower levels of legal immigration. FAIR publishes a wide variety of books, pamphlets, and educational materials, most of which are available for free.

Immigration and Naturalization Service (INS)
425 I St. NW
Washington, DC 20536
(202) 514-2000

The INS is the primary unit of the U.S. government that handles immigration issues. It provides hundreds of forms related to immigration applications, citizenship education and training, and related public information.

National Lawyers Guild, Inc.
National Immigration Project
14 Beacon St., Suite 506
Boston, MA 02108
(617) 227-7335

The National Immigration Project is a network of lawyers, law students, and legal workers who try to stop discrimination against immigrants. The organization is designed to "protect, defend, and expand the civil and human rights of all immigrants, regardless of their status in the United States." The project offers numerous publications, including the *Immigration Newsletter*, and instructions for representing immigrants in court.

Refugee Policy Group (RPG)
1424 Sixteenth St. NW, Suite 401
Washington, DC 20036
(202) 387-3015

RPG focuses on international and domestic refugees and related humanitarian issues. It publishes the *RPG Review* and a large number of books and papers covering all issues related to refugees.

United States Catholic Conference (USCC)
Migration and Refugee Services
1312 Massachusetts Ave. NW
Washington, DC 20005
(202) 541-3000

The USCC's Migration and Refugee Services helps to develop policy on migration, immigration, and refugee issues used by the United States to determine and analyze national policies. It operates 145 diocesan refugee resettlement offices throughout the country and helps to resettle thirty thousand or more refugees to the United States each year.

U.S. Committee for Refugees (USCR)
1025 Vermont Ave.
Washington, DC 20005
(202) 347-3507

USCR is a public information program of the American Council for Nationalities Service. It provides clear, objective information to the public, government, and the media to protect and assist refugees worldwide. USCR publishes a large number of papers about specific refugee conditions and publishes *The World Refugee Survey*, a comprehensive annual report on the world's refugees.

World Learning, Inc.
PO Box 676, Kipling Rd.
Brattleboro, VT 05302
(202) 258-3173

World Learning is an educational service that promotes learning and cultural exchange through its programs, which are the School for International Training, the Citizen Exchange and Language Programs, Projects in International Development and Training, and the U.S. Experiment in International Living. Through World Learning programs, U.S. students can, among other opportunities, live and work with refugees in foreign countries.

Suggestions for Further Reading

Brent Ashabranner, *The New Americans: Changing Patterns in U.S. Immigration*. New York: Dodd, Mead, 1983.

Leon F. Bouvier, *Immigration: Diversity in the United States*. New York: Walker & Company, 1988.

Warren Cohen, "The Millionaire Immigrants," *U.S. News & World Report*, June 10, 1991.

Carol Olsen Day and Edmund Day, *The New Immigrants*. New York: Franklin Watts, 1985.

Mark Dowie, "Bring Us Your Huddled Millionaires," *Harper's,* November 1991.

William Dudley, ed., *Immigration*. San Diego: Greenhaven Press, 1990.

Paul Glastris, "Thinking Straight About Immigration," *U.S. News & World Report*, May 20, 1991.

Alice J. Hall, "Immigration Today," *National Geographic*, September 1990.

John F. Kennedy, *A Nation of Immigrants*. New York: Harper & Row, 1964.

Lee Kravitz, "This Is Just a Waiting Place," *Scholastic Update*, October 18, 1991.

Richard Lacayo, "Give Me Your Rich, Your Lucky . . . ," *Time*, October 14, 1991.

John H. Lee, "Army Announces Plan to Illuminate Border," *Los Angeles Times*, September 10, 1992.

Katie Monagle, "They Ran for Their Lives," *Scholastic Update*, October 18, 1991.

William Steif, "Trapped on the Border," *The Progressive*, January 1992.

Works Consulted

Lawrence Auster, "The Forbidden Topic: Our Disappearing Common Culture," *National Review*, April 27, 1992.

Peter Brimelow, "Time to Rethink Immigration?" *National Review*, June 22, 1992.

Roy Simón Bryce-Laporte, ed., *Sourcebook on the New Immigration: Book II*. New Brunswick, NJ: Transaction, 1979.

Pastora San Juan Cafferty, Barry R. Chiswick, Andrew M. Greeley, and Teresa A. Sullivan, *The Dilemma of American Immigration: Beyond the Golden Door*. New Brunswick, NJ: Transaction Books, 1984.

Robert A. Carlson, *The Americanization Syndrome: A Quest for Conformity*. New York: St. Martin's Press, 1987.

Lawrence Eagleburger, "Refugee Admissions Proposal for FY 1992," *US Department of State Dispatch*, September 30, 1991.

Alberta Eiseman, *From Many Lands*. New York: Atheneum, 1970.

Nancy Foner, ed., *New Immigrants in New York*. New York: Columbia University Press, 1987.

Bill Frelick, "Who Is a Refugee?" *The World & I*, October 1992.

Jonathan Friedlander, ed., *Sojourners and Settlers: The Yemeni Immigrant Experience*. Salt Lake City: University of Utah Press, 1988.

John Fund, "Green Card," *The New Republic*, January 27, 1992.

Mark Gibney, *Strangers or Friends: Principles for a New Alien Admission Policy*. Westport, CT: Greenwood Press, 1986.

Jerry Gray, "Hudson County a Harbinger of a New Hispanic Influence," *The New York Times*, February 23, 1991.

Oscar Handlin, *The Uprooted: The Epic Story of the Great Migrations That Made the American People*. 1951. Reprint. Boston: Atlantic Monthly Press, 1973.

Donna Hrinak, "Restoring Democracy in Haiti: Persistence and Patience," *US Department of State Dispatch*, February 24, 1992.

Immigration and Naturalization Service, *1990 Statistical Yearbook of the Immigration and Naturalization Service*. Washington, DC: Government Printing Office, December 1991.

Kenneth F. Johnson and Miles W. Williams, *Illegal Aliens in the Western Hemisphere: Political and Economic Factors*. New York: Praeger Publishers, 1981.

Charles B. Keely, "Heating Up the Melting Pot," *The World & I*, October 1992.

Thomas Kessner and Betty Boyd Caroli, *Today's Immigrants, Their Stories: A New Look at the Newest Americans*. New York: Oxford University Press, 1981.

Richard Kolm, *The Change of Cultural Identity: An Analysis of Factors Conditioning the Cultural Integration of Immigrants*. New York: Arno Press, 1980.

Greta Kwik, *The Indos in Southern California*. New York: AMS Press, 1989.

Princeton N. Lyman, "FY 1993 Budget Request for Migration and Refugee Assistance," *US Department of State Dispatch*, March 23, 1992.

Brunson McKinley, "US Policy on Haitian Refugees," *US Department of State Dispatch*, June 15, 1992.

Jefferson Morley, "Gene McNary: Riding the Tiger of U.S. Immigration Policy," *Los Angeles Times*, May 5, 1991.

David Rieff, "Coming Apart: America and the New Immigrant Experience," *Los Angeles Times*, May 5, 1991.

David Rieff, "The New Face of L.A.," *Los Angeles Times Magazine*, September 15, 1991.

Karl Schoenberger, "Moving Between Two Worlds," *Los Angeles Times*, July 12, 1992.

Peter Schuck, "Coming Together: America and the New Immigrant Experience," *Los Angeles Times*, May 5, 1991.

Carl Shusterman, "Opening the Door for Immigrant Professionals," *Issues in Science and Technology*, Fall 1991.

Rita Simon, "Public Opinion," *The World & I*, October 1992.

Reed Ueda, "The Permanently Unfinished Country," *The World & I*, October 1992.

Edward Wakin, *The Immigrant Experience: Faith, Hope, and the Golden Door*. Huntington, IN: Our Sunday Visitor, 1977.

Index

About the Author

Kelly Clark Anderson is a historian and an award-winning book designer. She is a coauthor of numerous social studies textbooks and state histories. She graduated from Columbia College in Missouri and studied law and history at the University of Missouri.

Picture Credits